Don't Wait for Your Ship to Come In...

Swim Out to Meet It

DON'T WAIT FOR YOUR SHIP TO COME IN ...

SWIM OUT TO MEET IT

TOOLS AND TECHNIQUES FOR POSITIVE LASTING CHANGE

Dr Gary Wood

CAPSTONE

Dedicated to 10 November 2001

and 'Both Sides, Now', Republic Street and LP.

CONTENTS

ACKNOWLEDGEMENTS

I'd like to acknowledge the help and support I received along the way in writing this book.

Thanks to Sally Smith at Capstone-Wiley for commissioning this vessel and to John Moseley and Jenny Ng for getting it shipshape and sea worthy, and to Vicky Lyne who read over the first drafts of some of the chapters, made corrections and offered helpful suggestions. Thanks also to John Duggan at Sparks, and to Hamid Khan for well-timed albeit florid text messages. Thanks to all of my students and clients from whom I've learned a great deal too, especially the Psychological Studies students who took part in pilot personal development courses based on this book. Thanks to Al Thakur and Nitin Sharma for uplifting 'bright moments', to Dr Takeshi Fujisawa for his wonderful, inspirational cakes, to Carole Ramanouski and Sharon Steatham for the laughs and hearty cooked meals at The Waterloo and Bowie Shek for asking 'how's the book going?' every time he called.

A big thank-you to David Vann at the Birmingham School of Acting and all the great students on the Acting Summer School, especially the 'groovy gang': Jack Ramplin, Sarah-Louise Garrington, Alex Woodfield, Josh Wardell, and Jamelia Davis.

Thank also to Robert Biswas-Diener, for his insight and encouragement; Phyllis and Ian Pollock (Silva Method UK) for their encouragement and inspiration; Stephen Conlon for SFBT insights, Abigail Dixon press officer extraordinaire; BBC radio presenters Tony Wadsworth and Julie Mayer for providing me with some wonderful broadcasting opportunities as their 'tamed psychologist'. Thanks also to Dr Thomas Pagel for friendship, encouragement and impromptu media e-seminars. Thanks to friend and colleague Dr Petra Boynton for her support. Special thanks to Terry Chiu for inspiring me to be nostalgic for the future.

Finally, I dedicate this book to the memory of my grandparents: Nelly Florence Butcher, Clifford Bertram Butcher, Lillie Wood and William George Wood. I also dedicate it to my parents Shirley and William and to each and every member of my family, especially Tonie, Holly, Sean, and Kirsty ... and Tony ... and Tina ... and Matt ... and ... er. Oh yeah. Charlie.

THE INTRO

MAKING A SPLASH

Splish! There goes that coin in the wishing well. Splosh! There goes that message in a bottle! It's a start, but what next? Do I splash out on another lottery ticket? You too might have uttered the immortal phrase 'one day my numbers will come up' or 'one day my ship will come in'. Meanwhile, what do you do? In truth, we are all in the same boat as, more than ever before, we face a bewildering array of choices and decisions in our lives. Some of us may dream of a better income or better communication skills. Others may dream of a more satisfying job – or maybe just the ability to relax; or perhaps a healthy lifestyle, or to meet more friends. For some, it's the opportunity to make a contribution, whilst others may simply have a vague sense that things could be better. Whether you're feeling overwhelmed by opportunity or underwhelmed by routine, both feelings point to a need for change. We may know what we wish for, but what often eludes us is knowing exactly how and where to make a start. We all need a plan. Of course, sometimes it seems easier simply to wait and see what happens, trusting it all to the cosmic order and the fickle hand of fate. However, *Don't Wait For Your Ship to Come In ... Swim Out To Meet It!* is all about giving things a helping hand and, at the very heart of it, is the challenge:

It's your life, so take it personally!

Not surprisingly, as a psychologist, I figure that for real changes in the real lives of real people the answer lies in real psychology. By that I mean the vast body of evidence-based insights into what makes us tick and how we can tap into our inner pool of resources. This book offers a complete course – a personal development programme – guided by the three interweaving themes of *insight, ownership* and *action*. It contains all the essential tools and techniques, which will enable you to 'make a splash' and swim *with* the current rather than *against* it.

These themes – insight, ownership and action – are captured in the title *Don't Wait for Your Ship to Come In ... Swim Out To Meet It!*

- *Don't Wait* represents INSIGHT. Insight is the recognition that change is needed and that passively lying back and thinking of the cosmos is not the answer. This is based on deeper insights into what makes humans tick and, more specifically, insight into our personal values and strengths. Our ability to reflect on our present situation is a crucial part of how we learn.
- *It's Your Ship* represents OWNERSHIP. The logical step from recognizing that things must change is the mindset of taking things personally. The image of our ship coming in is another way of visualizing the achievement of our dreams and goals. Taking it personally emphasizes that it's not any old ship, it's the 'Owner Ship'! It's your cargo and your destination, which means it's time to take stock and plot your course.
- *Swim Out to Meet It* represents ACTION. 'Swimming out' is a metaphor for reaching out to your chosen goals. If you truly take your life personally, you will take action. 'Doing' is another crucial way in which we learn. We take action and we get feedback. Sometimes it's just what we expect, sometimes it's better, sometimes worse. However, a result is a result no matter what. With the new insights the feedback gives us, we can adjust course and steer ourselves in the direction of our goals.

You are undoubtedly your own ship's captain or your own lifeguard, and this book is intended as a lifeline – the training manual to help you become more effective in taking control. The themes of insight, ownership and action are the guiding lights by which you can transform mere wishful thinking into well-formed goals and, in turn, into manageable plans for concrete action. This will lead to positive outcomes and lasting change.

So let's consider what's different about this approach.

POSITIVE OUTCOME PSYCHOLOGY
Deep 'psy' diving

Don't wait ... Swim Out ...! distils the essential ingredients from the field of personal development, backed by evidence-based psychology, learning theory, teaching practice and coaching.

In bookshops, psychology titles are shelved in two sections: one for pop psychology and one for academic psychology. The academic ones often seem impenetrable to the average reader – you practically need an interpreter! There may be treasures to be found – but boy do you have to wade through a load of silt to get to them. On the other hand, the pop psychology titles are usually very accessible (hence their popularity) but frequently state the obvious or simply retread the same old ground – the psychological content is so diluted it's positively homeopathic! Both approaches can learn a lot from each other. Academic psychology would benefit from a bit of sparkle and it would certainly help if pop psychology had more depth.

What drives me as a social psychologist and a personal coach is the need to uncover those little psychological gems that can enrich our lives. I suppose that makes me a professional psychological treasure hunter – a dedicated deep 'psy' diver! Indeed, my research for this book involved wading through innumerable self-help books and immersing myself in personal development courses and self-help tapes, with a discerning, professional, psychological eye constantly on the lookout for those elusive pearls of wisdom.

You are holding the results in your hands. This book aims to put the 'pop' back into popular psychology coupled with insights from the academic world. It's a manual of P.O.P., that is, *Positive Outcome Psychology*. At the heart of it is the recognition that each of us has our own treasure chest of personal resources. We all gather information about the world and process it in pretty much the same way. Where we differ is in how we make sense of that information as we put our own individual spin on it. So it's true to say: each of us is unique – just like everyone else! At school we were crammed with facts and figures but rarely did anyone help us learn how to learn. Learning how we learn is a crucial aspect of personal development and is also at the heart of this book.

Beyond wishful thinking

The *positive outcome psychology* approach puts the emphasis on personal control over our lives. *Don't Wait… Swim Out…!* is all about being goal-led and action-focused, and the by-products of this ongoing process of development are increased self-esteem and self-confidence. This book is about the journey from abstract wishful thinking to concrete action – and ultimately to the successful realization of our goals – using the *psychological order* rather than the *cosmic order*!

Cosmic ordering is a self-help approach, like a non-religious form of prayer, that involves putting words and images out into the universe. If we do it right then our 'prayers' are answered. It's been around a long time in various guises and, in many ways, it's a good start. It recognizes the need for change (insight). Unfortunately it doesn't provide us with the tools to follow through (ownership and action). It's true that every act of creation begins with a thought but it is the act itself that gets us there, otherwise it's just wishful thinking. Waiting for promises from the stars merely instils a greater sense of helplessness. This book is about personal empowerment. For things to change, we have to do something!

I'd like to share a brief personal story and then consider two possible explanations for the results, the cosmic view and the psychological view.

RISE AND SHINE

Do you face the challenge each day to rise and shine when it's more tempting to stay in that warm bed? Rising is often a struggle we can manage but shining is maybe a step too far. To shine is to excel, to stand out from the crowd or maybe just to radiate an inner joy and appreciation for life itself. What? *Every* day?

My own challenge to rise and shine came as I neared the end of a particularly demanding term of teaching. As the end of the final week approached I pictured lying in bed on Saturday morning of the holiday sending out cosmic wishes and hoping the negativity would slip away. But, as the saying goes, 'a change is as good as a rest', so instead I decided to take ownership and choose some form of affirmative action to break the pattern. Call it an experiment; I just knew that I had to do something. So I made a few phone calls the night before and dragged myself out of bed at 5.30 a.m. on that cold Saturday morning and onto a train to London to attend a personal development course on creative visualization, *The Silva Method*.

Now, even though I had chosen to do it, I still felt vaguely resentful. However, as I settled in on that early morning 'ghost train' I experienced a change in perception. Although the coffee wasn't the greatest I still felt kind of grateful to be drinking it, even lucky. At that very moment as I looked out of the window I saw the sun begin to peek out from over the horizon. It somehow seemed significant that my change in attitude from resentment to gratitude heralded a brand new day, a new perspective on things. The sun rose at the very moment I began to shine! The knock-on effect was amazing. My writer's block shifted and I immediately began scribbling down these words. By the time I got to London, I felt like a different person. With my change in perception a burden became an opportunity. Without that change I would have missed the sunrise. So, what have you missed lately because 'your world' blocked your view?

By chance, during that same weekend, I discovered the book *Hidden Messages in Water* by Masuru Emoto. This wonderful book is a collection of photographs of frozen water crystals accompanied by the theory that water reflects emotions and intentions. The most beautiful photograph is of a frozen water crystal that has been exposed to the words 'love and gratitude'. Although the science doesn't hold water, the book served both as the inspiration for my New Year's card and as a great metaphor for how we live our lives: *take stock of what we have, and make a positive contribution.* Over that weekend I had turned things around by taking time to appreciate the small stuff and then taking action. My shift from resentment to gratitude helped change my perspective and made me more likely to see opportunities. After searching for a guiding metaphor for the book, I knew that I had found it: water.

It wasn't the cosmic order that turned things around for me. The answer is very down to earth: *insight, ownership* and *action.*

A VOYAGE ROUND YOUR MAP OF THE WORLD
Don't Wait ... Swim Out ...! mirrors the approach I use as a personal development coach. It's a partnership in which you provide the personal material to work on and I provide the strategy. So, let me explain a little about the layout of the book since information sinks in more easily if we know the context. Think of the times that you reach for the TV guide to get an idea of what an unfamiliar film is about. As soon as you know it stars Bruce Willis you immediately think 'Ah! It's a guns and vests movie'. You don't have to strain to work things out. In a similar way, the layout of this book represents the map and route for your personal voyage of discovery. Once you are familiar with the layout, you can focus on your issues.

The map
To gain the greatest benefit from this journey it will help if you 'suspend your disbelief' and work through it from beginning to end. Each chapter begins with a few quotations and a brief preview (dipping a toe) to set the scene. The main body of each chapter often includes exercises and quizzes, which should be tackled as you encounter them. Apart from these, there are a number of small 'personal experiments' throughout. These are, essentially, low-threat opportunities for you to test the water. As with any experiment there's no such thing as failure; you just receive feedback from the results. It's then up to you to apply these insights. To help you keep track of these experiments, I suggest you keep a learning journal, a

bit like a captain's log. Anything can go in here from notes about exercises, things you've tried, things you've read, things that worked and things that didn't. It's your own personal account of your learning. There are no right and wrong answers and it will be different for each of us. It's just about reflecting on what works for you, what doesn't work and why. To help out with this, each chapter concludes with an opportunity for reflection (think: *refl-action*), using the principles on *insight, ownership* and *action*.

So, if you haven't done so already, have a quick flick through the book to familiarize yourself with the layout. And now, let's look at the various ports of call in our voyage.

The route

Our journey is organized into three main parts to take on board the themes of insight, ownership and action. *Part One: From Insight to Ownership* contains four chapters with a theoretical emphasis as the groundwork for the practical tools and techniques. These chapters cover perception (Chapter One); learning (Chapter Two); values and attitudes (Chapter Three) and personal strengths (Chapter Four). Together they provide a good outline of how we process information, how we learn, how we make sense of the world, and insight into personal strengths and resources. In this way, you are set up for action.

Part Two: From Ownership to Action has an emphasis on practical tools and techniques. The four chapters in this section form a series of interlinking ideas, tools and techniques designed to help you change perceptions and take action with a series of personal experiments. Taking our lives personally inevitably involves making decisions and that is far easier from a position of calm rather than stress. Therefore, the first series of tools and techniques centres on the ability to relax (Chapter Five). From a position of calm we then take a look at goals (Chapter Six) and how we can transform the sketchiest of ideas into effective plans for concrete action and positive lasting change. The next two chapters focus on how we can support goal setting with the creative, strategic use of our imagination (Chapter Seven). In short, we concentrate on creating positive mental pictures to support goals and help develop skills. Having taken control of our mental pictures, we round off with *self-talk*. This is the running commentary that goes through our heads. Sometimes the things we say to ourselves can grind us down. In this chapter (Chapter Eight) we'll find out how to create language that is more supportive of our goals in life.

At this point, we have a balance of theoretical (part one) and practical knowledge (part two) using the themes of *insight, ownership* and *action* to create your own personal development *tour de force*.

Part Three: Less Distraction, More Action contains two chapters to round off this voyage. Chapter Nine is a trouble-shooting chapter, which explores the subject of self-sabotage. It considers our self-imposed obstacles and relates them back to the material covered in the previous chapters. Finally, thinking of our actions as ever-expanding ripples in a pool, Chapter Ten takes a leap to consider how we can make a difference to others and the implications affecting us.

The book offers conclusions and a list of learning resources to deepen the understanding gained from this journey.

Metaphors for positive, lasting change

For a guiding metaphor in reading and working through this book, think of the image of a stream. You will notice that a stream finds a way around obstacles. Sometimes it goes round the rock and occasionally, in time, it makes a hole and goes right the way through it. Think also about swimming through a pool strewn with obstacles. To get across we don't focus on the obstacles but on the spaces in-between and the way ahead. We are aware of the obstacles, but they are not our primary focus. The lesson, as each of us works on our personal development, is to have an understanding of the problem and an awareness of the obstacles but to focus on the solutions. We tend to follow our eyes. In short, we look where we want to go. You've probably seen a film with a scene involving someone dangling over the edge of a cliff. The rescue invariably shouts 'Don't look down! Grab my hand'. In this situation, focusing on the helping hand makes pretty good sense! So it's either oblivion or onwards and upwards, just like the mountaineer who focuses on the peak experience. I'm tempted to burst into a chorus of *River Deep, Mountain High* at this point. I'll resist.

Don't Wait … Swim Out …! won't leave you on hold, high and dry and waiting for change to mysteriously percolate through. Our wishful thinking provides the insight to reach our own positive outcomes, but our actions help us to grasp them! However, before we begin, let's indulge in a little wishful thinking.

MESSAGE IN A BOTTLE

Close your eyes and, in your imagination, write out your goals, dreams, wishes and ambitions on separate pieces of paper. Imagine rolling up these pieces of paper and stuffing them inside empty glass bottles. Still in your imagination push corks in the necks of the bottles, take them all to the edge of the ocean and thrown them in, one by one. Watch them drift out on the tide. Now go home and wait for the cosmos to grant your wishes.

Now, while you're waiting consider this: imagine that during the night, while you are asleep, all of your wishes are granted. You wake up tomorrow unaware that this has happened overnight. What are the first tiny signs that something has changed in your life? How will you go about testing your suspicions that something has changed? What will you be doing, saying or thinking differently? How will things be different if you implement one of those tiny changes right now? What do you think will happen if you help the change process along? That's what we intend to find out!

Gary Wood

part one:

FROM INSIGHT TO OWNERSHIP

Chapter One

NEW EYES: NEW LANDSCAPES

You, the viewing and the doing

> *If the doors of perception were to be cleansed everything would appear to [humankind] as it is, infinite.*
>
> William Blake
>
> *The real voyage of discovery consists not in seeking new landscapes but in having new eyes.*
>
> Marcel Proust
>
> *In the field of observation, chance favours only the prepared mind.*
>
> Louis Pasteur

DIPPING A TOE

Preview: In this chapter we ponder the basic principles of how we make sense of the world through the way in which we process information. Inevitably, how we view the world influences what we do in the world and vice versa. We consider the relationship between perception and experience and how we can use this as a basis for creating positive change.

SENDING OUT AN SOS

Our hopes, dreams and wishes are the compass readings for our ideal destinations. Knowing where we want to go is half the battle. The only thing we have to work out is the means to get there! The SOS message in the bottle is passive: 'save our souls'. We sit in hope and wait. But this is too important to trust to fate. So how different would things be if we decided to 'save our selves' by 'supporting our strengths' and 'seeking out solutions'?

At the close of the introduction I asked you to imagine that some magical changes had taken place in your life. So, what will those changes be? This deceptively powerful technique is a variation of *miracle question* used in solution-focused counselling. The aim is to engage our imagination in order to shift perceptions and concentrate attention on positive outcomes. This chapter is all about exploring your perceptions and the impact they have on the way you view the world, the way you live your life and how you learn.

Often we take for granted the complex mix of psychological processes which we use to go about our everyday lives. We all share a basic psychology of how we make sense of the world. There are certain principles to which we all adhere. On top of this we overlay our individual take on the world. As you read these words you are using your attention, your memory, perception and ability to make sense of language. At the same time as you tune into the words on the page you are filtering out unwanted noise and distractions. So, in order to make sense of things, our attention needs to be selective. In short we have a filtering system that is a mixture of shared values and individual perceptions. Our view of the world and of ourselves is shaped by what we pay attention to, what we allow to filter through and what we filter out.

Self-help books often pose the question: 'are we what we focus on?' This is another way of asking, 'are our lives shaped by attention and perception?' *Insight* into these basic processes will help you take *ownership* of the way you view the world and lead to *action* in support of your goals. This chapter aims to answer this question and will form the basis for exploring your own personal psychology in subsequent chapters of this section (learning style, values and strengths). So, let's begin by considering this process of selective attention.

YOU ONLY HEAR WHAT YOU WANT TO HEAR; YOU ONLY SEE WHAT YOU WANT TO SEE

The words of William Blake, in the opening quotation, suggest that we can change our view of the world if we clean up our perceptions. Everyday we filter our experience of the world by selectively tuning in and switching off. To get a better idea of this process, let's start by having a party.

The cocktail party phenomenon

Let's imagine you're on that ship you've been waiting for and you're having the time of your life. Picture a glamorous cocktail party and you're enjoying the most enthralling conversation with someone. You're laughing and joking and feel that you've known this person for years. You're totally at ease and absolutely oblivious to everything else going on around you. Amidst the cacophony of voices and the strains of an inebriated pianist, who sounds like he's playing the cracks, you are able to focus only on the sound of that silky, sensuous voice.

Those honeyed tones are simply music to your ears, which is more than can be said for that pianist! Oh yes, and if that wasn't enough, this person is drop-dead gorgeous, and flirting. You just know it's leading somewhere and you love every minute of it! Suddenly someone across the room just barely whispers your name. What happens next?

More than likely at the mention of your name your undivided attention will be more than divided. You will totally switch your concentration, cutting the drop-dead gorgeous one dead in mid-sentence and turning around to see who's talking about you. And you wonder why you always strike out at cocktail parties! Don't worry; you're not alone. Chances are, we'd all do the same!

First discussed by cognitive psychologist Colin Cherry in the 1950s, it's known as the *cocktail party phenomenon*. It shows our attention is selective and that we filter information based on personal relevance. Names have a high priority. Just the mere mention of ours can make us switch, even if we're having fun and flirting. So what are you switching off right now?

Exercise: background noise
Pause for a moment and tune in to the sounds and sensations that you are filtering out.

- *Look around and just focus on the ordinary things.* Scrutinize your environment. What can you see that you have overlooked before? Have you spotted something that needs painting or cleaning? What about an interesting pattern in the wallpaper you've never noticed before? Look at a clock. Are there people around you hadn't noticed? What else?

NEW EYES: NEW LANDSCAPES

- *What can you hear now that you weren't paying attention to before?* Is it the ticking clock, the dull roar of the air conditioning, church bells or a car alarm in the distance? Can you hear the traffic, a dog barking or children playing? Can you hear the hissing of a bus's breaks, an aeroplane overhead or the siren of one of the emergency services? What else?

- *Now bring your attention to sensations and feelings.* What do you notice? May be you have suddenly become aware of the feel of your clothes, the pressure of the seat, or aches and pains. Maybe it's a cold draught you'd been ignoring. What else?

- *Now focus on your other senses of taste and smell.* What do you notice? Are there food smells drifting by? Can you smell perfume or body odour? Is there a taste in your mouth and do your teeth feel clean? What else?

This simple exercise demonstrates how we can subtlety change our experience of the world by what we focus on. Routinely we tune in to what's important to us and tune out what's not. However, sometimes we just get into the habit of not fully engaging with life.

OK, switch back to the book, enough noise and distraction!

RE-COGNITION

We actively transform the information we receive through our senses. We don't just passively soak up information; we do something with it to make it personally relevant and useable. One of the main features of this is that we just focus on the most important parts and filter out the 'noise'. This is known as *selective attention*. We experience this when we become engrossed in a book or television and block out the distractions. We become oblivious to what's going on around us. It is only when a person uses our name or asks 'do you fancy some chocolate?' that we switch attention. So, the next time you get annoyed when people ignore you, remember it's just the result of selective attention. Well, either that or they are downright rude!

Attention and perception belong to the realm of cognitive psychology, the study of how we process information and make sense of the world. We refer to these processes whenever we use the word 'recognition'. In effect we go through the same process that got the information into our heads in the first place. It's not the sexiest area in psychology but it contains a wealth of material on how to make learning easier and more effective. As a student I learned, that with the help of some basic principles I could study smarter rather than harder, if I went with the natural flow of my innate abilities.

The fact is that our attention span is a lot shorter than we think. We can only pay full attention to something for about 20 minutes. After that it becomes more difficult to maintain optimum attention and retain information. This means that if we have a long task to tackle then short intensive bursts of activity are the most effective. This was music to my ears; it meant more breaks *and* it was psychologically justified!

As the saying goes: 'when we know better we do better'. By working with this simple psychological insight I took greater ownership of my perception of what studying for exams meant to me. It ceased to be so boring and my recall of information improved dramatically. Essentially, I had stumbled across a simple law of human perception and experience: *the viewing influences the doing*, and vice versa.

Our perceptions change our experience of the world which in turn reshapes our perceptions, and on it goes. So let's continue by looking more closely at our selective attention.

THE COST OF SELECTIVE ATTENTION

So why is our attention so selective? And why is the human attention-span so short? To answer this I want you to imagine what it would be like if you had to process every bit of information that came your way. Well, either it would cause a massive information overload or else our brains would need to be huge. This means bigger heads and chaos at weddings with hats the size of ocean liners!

Instead we have a limited capacity to process information, and we're hard-wired for speed and *cognitive economy*. Each piece of information to which we pay attention incurs a processing cost and we only have limited energy. Therefore, we need to make sure it's going to be worth it. This selectivity is based on what is personally relevant to us to maintain consistency in our world.

However, one of the pitfalls is that if we are too selective then we block out new information. Therefore we have a competing drive for novelty. In effect, we are torn between the two. On one hand we have 'go with what you know' and on the other hand it's 'Hey, over here! Look at me!' This helps maintain the balance between fresh input and what we are used to.

Our need for novelty also helps out in the area of cognitive economy. Information about the world comes to us through our five senses (sight, hearing, touch, taste and smell). Each sense has a reservoir of 'attention energy' assigned to it, rather like a rechargeable battery. If we focus on one task that requires one particular type of attention, and for extended periods of time energy, we tend to experience fatigue. More effort is required to 'squeeze out' the processing power and so we tire or make errors. This is why simple, repetitive tasks are more tiring than ones with variety. In order to recharge our resources all we need to do is take a short break, or switch to a different type of task with an emphasis on a different sense. A change is indeed as good as a rest. So rather than being easily distracted, our brains are actually hard-wired for distraction. And no, it's not an excuse!

If you cast your mind back to when you were an infant, think of the incredible amount of information you acquired in a very short space of time. Alongside that, you were trying to gain a sense of predictability in the world even whilst you were captivated by novelty. If we forsake novelty and become too set in our ways then we limit our options for new learning experiences. As a result we become inflexible and closed-off and tend to respond to the world in predictably comfortable ways. If the novelty takes over we never settle, commit or achieve anything. The push and pull of these competing demands helps to maintain a productive balance.

Advertisers are expert in manipulating messages to grab our attention with the aim of getting us to select their message from amidst the competition with a hope that it will influence the choices we make. They hit us with a double whammy. They appeal to our need for novelty and our need for predictability or consistency in the world. Their messages tend to be bigger and brighter, will play on creating contrasts, may take us by surprise, but will also play to our emotions and to our sense of values. So the next time you feel tempted to buy something you can't afford, consider which buttons are being pressed. It will certainly help you to work out the financial cost of your selective attention.

Our perceptions are shaped by what we've paid attention to. Working together, attention and perception shape our view of the world.

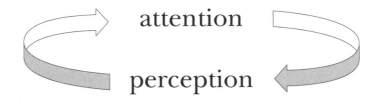

New information is based, to a large degree, on personal relevance. We are, in effect, cognitive cherry pickers – collecting information that is most relevant to us and filtering out the rest. Based on culture, background, learning, mood, context, time of day and individual idiosyncrasy, personal experiences, motivations, likes and dislikes, we continue to shape and re-shape our view of the world based on what we value and what we're used to. In effect we only see what we want to see and hear what we want to hear! The rest gets filtered out. This creates what is known in psychology as a *perceptual set* (similar to everyday 'mindset'). This set of perceptual filters is like security staff at your private party. Information only gets in if it's 'on the list' or if it has the element of surprise. Popular psychology often states that it is our perception that creates the reality and, to a large extent, this notion is supported by academic psychology.

Let's consider the content of our perceptual filters in greater detail.

FRAME OF MIND: EYE OF THE BEHOLDER
'I filter therefore I am'

We take for granted many of the factors that influence our perceptions mainly because we spend very little time thinking about them. Some factors such as gender, race and attractiveness shape the entire course of our lives and we are never allowed to forget them. Invariably they set up a lifelong chain of expectations in terms of our behaviour, how we relate to others, our sexual encounters, prospective partners, economic prosperity and even our personality. And although we may not be able to change barriers in our lives, we can certainly change our perception of them.

Let's take a more detailed look at the major perceptual filters that shape our lives.

Filters in a major key

The groups and categories to which we belong colour our perceptions and shape our view and experience of the world. Let's consider these major perceptual filters. So, for each of the following categories ask yourself these questions:

- What are the benefits and limitations of belonging to this category/group?
- If you 'switched sides' or belonged to another group, what would be different for you?
- How would this change or affect your view of the world?

- How would switching groups affect your choices and opportunities, for better or worse?
- How does belonging to a particular group affect your attitudes and values?
- Would your values change if you could switch groups?

Gender (being a masculine man, a feminine woman or something else)	
Culture and ethnicity	
Sexuality (gay, straight, bisexual, hetero, homo, or defies classification)	
Age (young, older, old, middle-aged)	
Social and peer groups (and any other group that you feel defines your identity)	

Now imagine reading the newspaper, in particular some hot political issue. How will these factors impact on your views? Will some pieces of information be more important to you than others?

Now consider these following factors too. How would your view of the world change if things had been or were different now?

Upbringing, childhood and adolescence	
Education (type and level)	
Home and environment	
Health	
Wealth	

Now consider:

- How do all of these things contribute to your values and what you stand for?
- What do you hold dear?
- What social issues are important to you?
- How do your values contribute to your view of the world?
- How has your view of the world changed over time?
- With whom would you swap places for a day to have the most dramatic change on your view of the world?

To get an idea of how perceptions change over time we only have to consider the field of fashion. Our old photograph albums provide ample evidence. I'm guessing that you have pictures in there that make you squirm with embarrassment. I know I do. What was I thinking at the time? Fashions come and go and with them our sense of what looks good. What was cutting edge at the time now looks like a fashion disaster until everything goes full cycle and the disasters become next season's new thing. Fashion is just a matter of perception. It's just that sometimes we have to stand back a little to gain a sense of how our perceptions are altered.

As if that wasn't enough to contend with, we have a whole set of minor filters that colour our perceptions.

Filters in a minor key

Mood swings, different situations, the time of day, and biological cycles all colour our perceptions and experience to varying degrees. Added to these are likes, dislikes, motivations, wants and needs, and so on. Take time to work through these questions and make notes in your journal before moving on.

Our minds do indeed play tricks on us as we distort perceptions in line with our needs such as hunger and thirst and the need for security. You've probably seen cartoons where hungry characters see everything in the shape of food. This also happens in the real world. Research has shown that hungry people perceive food photographs as brighter than neutral ones. Children draw larger pictures of Santa before Christmas as compared with pictures after. Our sugar levels fluctuate throughout the day and this affects our mood which means we may react differently to jokes or comments from others. Then there are the effects of confidence, self-esteem or a myriad of other personality factors. Individual physical characteristics such as height, weight, hair colour, eye colour, and attractiveness may also have an impact on our perceptions and the people with whom we interact. Other people's perceptions of us affect our perceptions of ourselves. This may affect our actions which in turn affect our perceptions (the viewing–doing cycle). It's a complex process. It's not just beauty that's in the eye of the beholder. Reality is too!

All this means that we are primed to respond automatically. Our perceptual filters create the expectation and trigger pre-packaged sets of responses all ready to go. Much of the time our filters serve us well, but if fresh input never gets through we jump to conclusions based on prior expectations. We fill in the missing gaps, simply seeing what we want to see.

Self-fulfilling prophecy

We adjust our behaviour in line with the expectations of others and of ourselves. When we use the phrase 'self-fulfilling prophecy' it is most often in a negative context. We internalize expectations or predictions and then set out to make sure they come true. For instance, we may predict that we will fail at a test and then unwittingly sabotage events or our behaviour to make sure the prophecy comes true! These expectations can be so powerful that they can cause us to deny the evidence of senses.

Consider an everyday example when you're late for work and say to yourself 'I bet I won't be able to find my keys'. That prediction turns out to be true and it certainly doesn't help when some bright spark asks 'Where did you leave them?' Of course you first looked in the place where you always leave them and they weren't there. So you continue frantically to upturn the whole house in search of the keys. In desperation you return to the place where you thought you left them. They aren't there and so more frantic upturning follows. You take a moment to pause and say to yourself emphatically 'Yes they are where I usually put them. They must be.' Miraculously you return to the place you had searched a dozen times before and there they are. They had been there all along!

Given the power of perceptions and expectations over such a mundane task as finding our keys, just imagine the impact when faced with our goals. This example is particularly pertinent to me as I write these words. I reached a stage where my head was spinning (not literally, just metaphorically; it wasn't that distressing). I was stuck on an early chapter and said to myself, 'I'll never get this right'. Sure enough I continued *not* to get it right. Knowing that I was stuck a friend sent me a text (SMS) message. It read:

> The day will come when
> u have ur epiphany, and
> then shores of paper
> will be awash with
> the inks of your heart.

Yes he does speak like that! The message made me LOL (text speak: 'laugh out loud'). Something so simple put a smile on my face and created a shift in perception. I resolved to get up early the next day and finish the chapter. By 10 a.m. the next day, simply by moving a few paragraphs around, the chapter began to work.

So, what limiting attitudes, beliefs, perceptions and expectations do you have about your own ability? Have you set yourself up for failure before you even start? Do you tell yourself 'If I don't expect much out of life, I'll never be disappointed?'

WYSIWYG

Are we defined by what we focus on? From a psychological perspective, the poet Horace's hypothesis that 'Life is a matter of expectation' is largely true. WYSIWYG (pronounced 'wizzy-wig') is a computer acronym meaning **W**hat **Y**ou **S**ee **I**s **W**hat **Y**ou **G**et. In other words what you see on the screen is what you will get when you print it out. Our perceptual filters work rather like the automatic features in a computer word-processing program. These features try to predict what you want to do based on a mixture of what most people want to do, and on past performance. Type one bullet point and before you know it your page looks like a shoot-out in a Tarantino movie. However, knowing a little more about computers enables you to switch off the automatic features or create new features of your own. You can shape the computer's automatic features to your needs. The same applies to predictive text on mobile phones. When you first get your phone it tries to guess what you want to type on the basis of the most commonly used words. As you go along you can add new words into the dictionary. In doing so, predictive features reflect more accurately the way you use language and your view of the world. Each chapter of this book – following the principles of *insight, ownership* and *action* – aims to help you consider the predictive features of your perceptual filters, challenge them and, where appropriate, make changes to get your perceptions working for you, not against you.

THE 'YES BUT' JUNKIE
Maybe the views expressed so far are a little bit too Pollyanna for you. You may argue 'Yes but ... it won't work in the real world.' To which I reply 'Yes but ... I'm talking about the *perceived* world.' Lost your keys recently? Did they disappear in the real world only to reappear in the first place you looked? No, of course not.

'Yes but' means NO! The perceptual shutters are down to solutions and locked into problems. Give the 'yes but' junkie a 99 per cent solution and they'll wrestle you to the ground over that elusive one per cent! And for as long as the 'yes but' filter is switched to maximum, there will never be any possibility of solutions. Whatever you choose to focus on, you'll get more of it. Problem seekers are rewarded with ever mounting problems. Solution seekers are rewarded with solutions.

The aim of this book is to balance the need for familiarity and predictability with fresh input and perspectives. The tools and techniques are designed to switch off automatic 'yes but' filters, in order to give our solution-seeking filters a chance. It's not a book of answers but rather a book of possibilities. You apply the tools and get your own answers. You can start this process at anytime by asking the simple question: 'How would this work for me?' This book is a blueprint for you to create a *personal development* system that lives up to its name: *you develop as you develop it!*

So, to return to the question of, 'Are we what we focus on?', well, we have seen that attention and perception, to a large extent, shape our view of ourselves and of our world. This affects how we behave and how we think, which in turn affects our attention and perception. This circular process goes on and on. The good news is that we can interrupt this cycle and actively take control of what we pay attention to. This will have a knock-on effect in terms of how we view ourselves and our world. So, let's get personal and put this to the test with the first experiment.

A PERSONAL EXPERIMENT IN ATTENTION AND PERCEPTION

This simple experiment is designed to test the idea that we can retune our filters and change the way we view the world. For the experiment you'll need your journal or notebook.

Gratitude and anticipation

1   Before you go to sleep tonight write down a minimum of three things that have happened today for which you are grateful. In effect you are counting your blessings.

2   Now add three people to whom you are grateful today, for whatever reason. It can be a lover, a friend or the person who works at the corner shop.

3   Repeat for the next 27 nights.

4   When you awake tomorrow, list a minimum of three things you are looking forward to during the day (however small). It could be a trip to the gym, a nice cappuccino or getting to grips with a new project.

5   Repeat this for the next 27 days.

The aim is to continue this practice for 28 consecutive nights and days. The duration is arbitrary, but it needs to be long enough for you to gauge the results. So, if you can't manage a month, try it for at least one week. Don't worry if you miss a day; just start again until you have completed the experiment. At the end of the 28 days read back over your journal or notebook. Did the experiment have any effect on the way you view your life and the world in general? Were you able to exert control over what you focused on? Do you think you might feel differently had you spent 28 days focusing on negative things? If you focus on gratitude and anticipation then you will notice more things for which you have to be grateful and focus on the things to which you look forward. This is only the starting point for creating positive outcomes and lasting change. It's a way of tuning in on new possibilities, new landscapes and new horizons.

NEW HORIZONS

Nothing broadens the mind like travel. One of the main reasons is that it allows us to grasp how other people in other

NEW EYES: NEW LANDSCAPES

countries make sense of the world. We may find foreign customs fascinating or frustrating. However, by travelling we hold a mirror up to our mental filters and learn something new about ourselves. So, the next time you think you can't afford that holiday, you have another reason to try to make it happen. 'Darling I really *do* need that world cruise this year – how else will I explore the limitations of my perceptions?' It's worth a try.

For the time being, however, you may have to settle for the voyage of discovery in this book.

DRYING OFF

Review: In this chapter we have pondered the question 'Are we defined by what we focus on?' We have considered the concepts of attention and perception, their roles in shaping our view of the world and how we relate to it. In short, the viewing shapes the doing and vice versa. On the one hand, our perceptual filters help to focus our attention to process information quickly and economically, homing in on the stuff with greatest personal relevance. On the other hand, the downside is that we run the risk of missing fresh input when we need a new perspective on things. We may just end up getting more of the same. Insight from cognitive psychology shows that we can intervene and retune or reprogramme our perceptual filters to our advantage.

In the next chapter we deepen our understanding as we consider more psychological principles of learning.

REFLECTION (*REFL-ACTION*)

1 **INSIGHT** (*Don't wait*): What are the three most important things you learned in this chapter?

(i)

(ii)

(iii)

2 **OWNERSHIP** (*It's your ship*): What impact has this had in terms of the way you think about your accountability for your life and goals?

3 **ACTION** (*Swim out to meet it*): What action will you take (*don't wait*) to make a positive change in your life? What personal experiment might you conduct to produce feedback and insight?

Chapter Two

SWIMMING LESSONS

Feedback not failure

You could not step twice into the same rivers; for other waters are ever flowing on to you.

Heraclitus

A thinker sees his own actions as experiments and questions – as attempts to find out something. Success and failure are for him answers above all.

Friedrich Nietzsche

I am not afraid of storms, for I am learning how to sail my ship.

Louisa May Alcott

DIPPING A TOE

Preview: In this chapter we'll look at how we learn, and in particular, the value of viewing failure as feedback. We examine the basic building blocks of learning and consider the idea of conducting personal development experiments.

MOVING ON

We live and we learn. As part of a lifelong information stream that constantly changes, we live in a state of flux, adapting and learning as we go. If there's one thing we can rely on to be constant in our lives, it is change! We continue to learn throughout our lives, whether we like it or not. Sometimes the learning comes easy. Sometimes we learn the hard way. We cannot halt the flow of new information, nor stand still. We can only learn to channel it. Ultimately, it's in our own best interest to take control of that learning. Sociologist Alvin Toffler, in his classic book on change: *Future Shock*, argues that it is our ability to learn, unlearn and relearn that distinguishes us above all else. Perception plays a key role in the learning process and we can view setbacks as failures or more productively as feedback.

So, this chapter will consider the basic building blocks of learning, our individual learning preferences and the value of role models and modelling roles, and other cognitive abilities. Owning these insights and putting them into practice is a crucial part of the blueprint for creating positive, lasting change. We begin with the learning cycle.

YOUR LEARNING CYCLE

We are all psychologists in the way we learn as we begin with 'educated guesses' (theories) about the world, put our hunches to the test and get feedback. With these new insights we either confirm our original theories or, more often than not, adjust the theory and repeat the learning process ... and on it goes. The beauty of this approach is that we can start out with a vague question in a more tentative way, such as 'I wonder what would happen if I do this?' The results provide feedback to refine the questions. We can then start asking more specific questions. In this way we get to home in on what works for us, under which conditions, and then eliminate what doesn't work. With an experiment there is no failure, just feedback. So, let's go back to the beginning and see how our first steps in learning illustrate this process.

Baby's first steps

The first time a baby attempts to walk, it topples over and lands on its bottom! The baby may even cry at the shock of the impact. So, what's a baby to do? Give up, try again, or try something slightly different? Well, by this time the baby already has a working idea of what to do. Based on observation, upright seems to be a good start. So after the momentary setback, with the benefit of a little reflection baby is ready to try again. 'If I shift my weight across to here and do this with my arm, then that just might work', thinks baby. So after shifting its weight and doing the arm thing, it's not long before baby's rear end is contemplating the floor again! After further reflection, it's decided that the arm thing was a winner, so a bit more of that, but a bit less of the weight-shift thing. On and on goes the process of contemplating, refining and testing. Sometimes there's notable progress and at other times it seems a little slow; nevertheless, the process keeps moving forwards. Contrast this with the less successful approach of the common housefly.

One day I'll fly away

Imagine there's a fly in your house. If that offends you then imagine it's in my house! Not being blessed with a sophisticated processing system, the fly thinks that as it can see through the window, it must be able to fly through it. Of course it hits the window. Unlike the baby, the fly doesn't reflect or adjust its approach. On and on it goes repeating the same mistake, head-butting the glass, even though there's an open window close by.

So, full marks to both the fly and the baby for incredible persistence, but bonus points to the baby for using the feedback and knowing when to try something different.

Personal experiments

Now, human beings are much smarter than flies. Compare diets for a start. However, sometimes when we are tired or frustrated we behave just like the fly, trying the same thing over and over again. And, when it doesn't work, we try it some more. We temporarily forget the 'feedback and adjust' approach we used as babies. All babies are little scientists performing experiments. That's how they manage to learn so much in such a short time. The personal experiments approach to learning gets us out of 'fly mode' and back into efficient 'baby mode'. Babies learn; flies use your food as their lavatory. Who do you want as your role model?

It's often repeated in self-help books that if what you're doing isn't working then try something else. Another self-help favourite is 'if you always do what you've always done, you'll always get what you've always got'. Novel inputs and the resulting feedback help create shifts in perception. The same old feedback maintains the perceptual status quo. The personal experiment approach works because it fits in with theories of how humans learn. We learn by a cycle of trial and error, reflection and adjustment.

Here's a basic layout of how to conduct these personal experiments.

Hypothesis: *What exactly do you want to find out? For instance, will it make a difference to your outlook if you conduct the gratitude and anticipation experiment for 28 days?*

What will I do? When? *Set out exactly what it is you are going to do.*

What resources will I need? *Decide whether you need any resources, such as a notepad or a supply of forms (see appendix).*

Do I need anyone to help me? If so, who and how? *Sometimes you may need to include others or enlist their help. Give details here.*

What are the results (feedback)? *This is where you assess the results. You get that all-important feedback.*

What are my conclusions? *You decide whether or not the results support the original hypothesis. Did you get a positive result, a negative or a partial one?*

What are the implications for future personal experiments? *What insights have you gained from the experiment?*

What will I do next? *How will you use the feedback for future personal experiments?*

Feedback, failure and the learning cycle
The research cycle in psychology (as in any science) is very much the same as a baby's learning cycle. As you see from the diagram of this cycle, there are four stages.

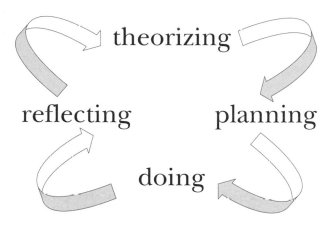

In their research, learning theorists Peter Honey and Alan Mumford argue that different people have a tendency to start at particular points based on their individual learning style (we'll discuss this in Chapter Four on personal strengths) or on the demands of a given situation. The whole thing is a feedback loop. It's feedback if you get the result you want and it's feedback if you don't. What is significant about this approach is that there is no *intrinsic* failure beyond the failure to use the feedback. We can also link the learning cycle to the principles underpinning this book. Reflection and theory correspond to *insight*, planning corresponds to *ownership* and *action* is common to both.

So, let's go back to the basics of how we learn.

THE BUILDING BLOCKS OF LEARNING

Throughout our lives we use the same basic building blocks of learning. In psychology there are three main principles think ACE:

(i)   Learning by Association (known as 'classical conditioning'),
(ii) Learning by Consequence (known as 'operant conditioning'), and
(iii) Learning by Example (known as 'modelling').

Taken together the ACE principles cover just about everything, and an understanding of how we learn can provide valuable insights for personal motivation and development. So let's consider these learning principles.

Association – classical conditioning: it's a dog's life

We learn by making links and associations between objects, ideas, thoughts, feelings, emotional states and events. As time goes by we make increasingly complex patterns of association. In psychology this process is known as *classical conditioning*. We owe this psychological insight to the eminent Nobel Prize winning Russian physiologist, Ivan Pavlov, and his work on digestion. He is best known for his research with dogs. However, his findings have since been generalized to just about every other species including humans.

It was observed that Pavlov's dogs salivated at the mere sight of food. In a series of experiments it was also demonstrated that if a bell was rung at the same time as the food was presented, eventually the dogs would salivate merely at the sound of the bell. In short, the dogs had learned to associate the bell with the mouth-watering food. The bell triggered the same response (salivation) in the absence of food. The same thing happens to humans too. Our mouths water just by watching TV cookery programmes. The smell of food as we pass a takeaway will cause associated memories to pop into our heads. We can hear a piece of music and it may cause us to feel happy or sad on account of associated memories. Comfort food works on the same principle. When we feel down and reach for the cake, chocolate or ice cream, it is not just the taste we enjoy, but also the pleasant memories and feelings we associate with these foods. The pleasant memories displace the unpleasant ones, for a little while at least.

Maybe there are some situations that fill you with dread. Is there a goal or ambition that you're not getting on with, or a task you're putting off? By considering the unpleasant associations with these tasks and goals you might find that you're replaying an event from your past. Do you associate the task with negative emotions such as boredom, resentment or fear? Awareness of these associations can affect your motivation, a factor on which we reflect in the next chapter. In the meantime, let's consider another type of basic learning.

Consequence – operant conditioning: better and better

We tend to repeat behaviours that have positive consequences and avoid those that don't. In effect, our behaviour is shaped by rewards and punishments, pleasure and pain. In psychology this learning by consequences is known as *operant conditioning*.

This insight was gleaned from a long list of somewhat cruel experiments on various animals, including rats, cats and pigeons. Using various contraptions involving levers, food pellets and electric shocks, a number of principles were discovered. Researchers waited patiently until a pigeon pressed a lever, which delivered a food pellet. This reward served to reinforce the behaviour and increase the likelihood that it would be repeated. In effect, we repeat behaviours for which we are rewarded. This reward is known as a *positive reinforcement*. By gradually making the rewards dependent on increasingly complex combinations of lever pressing, the birds were conditioned to perform intricate patterns of behaviour.

The more distasteful aspects of the experiments involved using electric shocks to observe the effects of punishment. It was found that as a consequence of punishment, patterns of behaviour could be reversed (and lever pressing ceased). Switching back to rewards, behaviours could be conditioned again. It's part of science to repeat experiments, making minor refinements. More experiments equals more feedback. The same can be said as we apply this principle to our personal development. If at first we don't succeed then use the feedback and try again!

The concepts of negative reinforcement and punishment are often confused. Negative reinforcement occurs when a person or animal performs a desired action to get something unpleasant to cease. For example, the experiment switches off a loud piercing alarm when a desired action is performed. It's the 'anything for a quiet life' approach, rather like when we put off unpleasant tasks until the stress becomes too much. The stress becomes worse than the task itself and so we do the task to put an end to the stress.

The principles of operant conditioning (learning by consequence) shape our behaviour, as we continue to make increasing approximations towards a goal. It's a matter of trial and feedback. Overall, psychological research shows that reward works better than does punishment. It's far more effective to reward those behaviours we want repeated and ignore the behaviours we want to go away. So, next time your child rolls on the floor at the supermarket checkout wanting chocolate, if you give in, you reward the bad behaviour! Instead, reward them after you leave the supermarket only if they have behaved.

Let's consider the concept of behaviour shaping in greater detail. As babies we uttered our first unintelligible sounds. The unreserved glee and praise from people around meant that we were sure to repeat them. However, in time, adults gave us more specific feedback to correct us, with the hope of getting us to say a recognizable word. The gurgling didn't get such enthusiastic responses but as soon as we uttered anything that even faintly resembled a real word, the glee returned. This encouraged us to repeat the new sound. Closer approximations to the target word elicited praise until we actually said a real word. Eventually after much ecstatic praising and coaching, 'Ugh ooh goo gah moo poo' becomes 'Me wanna drin drin'. This in turn becomes 'Hey I'm thirsty. Get me a drink' which in turn provokes the response 'You're old enough to get it yourself, and isn't it about time you moved out and got a place of your own?'

With learning by consequence (operant conditioning) we see the same approach of continual development modelled by the learning cycle. Consequences form the basis of motivation.

We can divide sources of motivation into two main types: external and internal. External motivators come from our surroundings; they may be tangible like chocolate or money, or less solid things such as praise, compliments or hugs. The big question is: what motivates us when the supply runs out? All too often we rely on external reinforcement to motivate us. However, the well of internal motivators such as our values and strengths does not run dry. They provide a stable and endless supply of motivation. It's just a matter of tapping into it. We'll consider motivation in greater depth throughout the book as we explore *values* (Chapter Three), *strengths* (Chapter Four) and *goals* (Chapter Six).

For the time being, it's enough for you to ponder the question of what motivates you. Right now, we are going to look at the third basic building block of learning.

Example – modelling roles (and role models)

We routinely use the phrase 'role models' to describe the way we follow the example set by other people. This is recognized as one of the key building blocks in psychology. Not surprisingly it is known as *modelling*.

Going back to the time when we first started to develop language, we did so by a mixture of operant conditioning (behaviour shaping) and by copying other people. Any action that we observe in others and attempt to imitate is modelling. It's a valuable strategy because it also lets us see the consequences of actions without trying them out for ourselves. This is known as vicarious learning. This means we can learn by the successes and mistakes of others.

Selectivity is the key when modelling. We need to cherry-pick and mix just those qualities and behaviours that we consider worthwhile. So when choosing a role model, it isn't necessary to take the whole package. Just isolate what you need.

Often we observe someone who makes a skill look effortless and assume they are gifted or born that way. As a social psychologist, I consider the emphasis always to be more on learning than on inherited skills. Many of our skills develop because we were rewarded in early life. Rewards (praise) caused us to repeat them and this practice made perfect. As our level of skill increases, just doing it becomes its own reward. This makes us feel good about ourselves and so we do it even more! So, when we see someone who appears to be a natural, we can be sure that a lot of learning by consequence helped the process along. What this means for us is that we can take any quality, skill or behaviour and observe someone who has it or excels at it. This can be anything from confidence to communication skills, business success to academic success, or dancing to sporting activity. We can model anything.

People tend to have scripts by which they reproduce skills, it's just that they are so well practiced that the scripts have become internalized and automatic. In order to uncover these scripts, all we need to do is to observe our role model in action. As we watch we begin to uncover the key steps and stages. Better still, it helps if we can ask them to talk us through what they do, how they feel, their thoughts, body posture, facial expressions, tone of voice and so on. Once we have the key components it's just a matter of putting them together and applying the learning cycle. With feedback and practise we adjust and improve until we get it right.

So, pause for a moment and think about what behaviours and skills you would like to acquire or goals you would like to achieve. Then, think of someone who has succeeded.

Behaviour/skill/goal	Role model

In preparation for the chapter on goal setting, begin by observing your role model and making a note of the key steps, stages and qualities that you need to emulate. This will become your script for positive outcomes.

So, now let's turn our attention to how we develop concepts and 'scripts' for behaviours.

SCHEMA: A LITTLE PACKET OF KNOWLEDGE

Learning by association, consequence and example enables us to form generalized packets of knowledge about the world. We begin with broad, vague ideas and later add specific details and exceptions as we go along. Just try it for a moment. What is a fish? You will probably start with a general description of a fish before moving on to types of fish. As we gain more information we add more detail to the concept. This information all gets bundled up into a packet of knowledge. Every time we think of a fish, it triggers all the information. It's another cognitive shortcut for processing information. These packets of knowledge are called schemas (properly 'schemata' but lets not get too Latin about it).

We have schemas for just about everything from simple objects and concepts to patterns of behaviours such as how to fish. On top of this we connect all of these schemas. For instance, fishing is connected with fish, water, fishing nets, the ocean, boats, ships and so on. In effect we create a network of schemas. The more we access them, the fresher they stay.

We build a schema by going through the learning cycle and updating it from time to time, with different options. So, we develop slightly different versions for going to different types of restaurant. For some restaurants we need to make a reservation and for others we just turn up and point at the brightly lit picture and mutter 'I want that one'. We acquire schemas for just about everything in our lives. It is a quick and easy method of making sense of the world. We don't have to process every piece of information from scratch; we just have to trigger the closest schema (generalized packet of knowledge).

Let's consider a very basic example of how we build a schema for recognizing a dog and distinguishing it from other four-legged mammals. We begin by learning how to say the word 'dog' or 'doggy' with a vague attempt: 'durrgh'. As we receive feedback from others, we get better. Then we learn to associate the word 'doggy' with the sight of a furry thing with a leg at each corner. We then test out this new schema on anything that vaguely approximates the image we have. So if we see animal, we immediately burst into 'doggy doggy doggy'. If it happens to be a dog then the whoops of glee and approval reinforce this association. At this stage we have schema limited to only a few characteristics. We may not have learned that dogs come in different colours. Our existing schema may only include the colour black and if we see a white dog, then we take a chance and shout doggy again. After all it's furry and has a leg at each corner. With enthusiastic feedback we amend the schema (*note to self: doggies come in two shades, dark ones and light ones*). This process continues as we update the doggy schema for size, sound, different location and so on.

Now, there comes a time when the schema doesn't fit. You've shouted 'doggy doggy doggy' at the sight of a small, dark coloured, furry object with a leg at each corner and you're expecting an ovation, yet you get nothing. This time all you get is a 'No, that's a cat.' What a failure! I'll never shout 'doggy' again! Alternatively you take the feedback and make a mental note: cat is not dog; start new schema. Now you have two schemas to help you make sense of the world. At the house of the trendy relative you decide to show off your extensive knowledge of animal classifications and spy, in the middle of the room, a rather large furry object with a leg at each corner. You weigh up the odds and go for 'doggy doggy doggy'. Your efforts are met with looks of bewilderment or disapproval. However, this time you don't give up – you have another schema to hit them with.

Triumphantly you shout 'Cat, cat, cat!' What? No approval? Not doggy, not cat? Taken aback you await the feedback: 'No dear it's a designer coffee table!'

Learning by schemas has its benefits. Once we have learned a schema we can call it up in any similar situation. A few cues grab out attention, we access the relevant schema in our memory and we're ready to act. Schemas not only contain factual information but also our emotional responses. The downside of the speed of processing is that schemas are prone to errors. As they are a work in progress they contain default options. In effect we fill in the blanks based on what is most likely. This is very much like the predictive features on computer software and predictive text on telephones. Another problem with schemas is that we tend to filter the information that goes into them. It's another example of seeing what you've been primed to see. This is why sometimes two people can experience the same event and have a slightly different memory of it. So, next time you start arguing with someone over the fine detail, bear this in mind.

We even have schema for how to learn, *and* schemas for success and failure. For some people it will include the default value 'if at first you don't succeed: give up'! Your existing schema might be screaming 'failure, failure, failure' whereas the fresh input from this chapter tells you that it's feedback!

Our perceptual filters (previous chapter) play a crucial role in allowing our schemas to be updated. As babies and children we constantly update schemas and create new ones to fit new situations. As we age, we get set in our ways and stuck in our schemas. As lifelong learners, it's imperative that our schemas for learning remain relevant. So, we need to keep the learning cycle turning, and use the feedback to keep our schemas fresh.

So what's your schema for success and failure? What's the habitual script that you play? Are you harbouring self-limiting beliefs that there's no point in trying? Are you running a script that downplays your abilities and skills?

The following personal example demonstrates how my schema for transferable skills needed a little fine tuning.

PIGEON HOLES: A PERSONAL PERSPECTIVE

A downside of schema theory is that it tends to reinforce the view that knowledge is stored in discrete little boxes. Information can sometimes become context bound whereas insights gained in one area of our lives might be invaluable to lessons in an unrelated area.

Transferable skills

I'm forever encouraging my students to make connections across different topics rather than keeping information in discreet little boxes. The same can be said of life in general. In the field of Solution Focused Brief Therapy, there are techniques to encourage clients to transfer competency across context.

At the first meeting I attended of the Professional Speakers Association, the first new person I spoke to asked me if I had ever spoken in public. My immediate reaction was to say 'No', yet then followed this with examples of what I did for a living. As a psychologist, lecturer, coach, and broadcaster, I get paid to speak for a living. I was essentially operating a separate schema for what I did as a professional and what I thought a professional speaker did. Many people make the same mistake as I did. We all have core transferable skills but often don't make the connections and transfer skills from one context to another, and between one time and another.

'The show must go on'

Before I found my passion for psychology – during my wild and reckless youth – I was in several rock bands. It was a long time before I realized how valuable those years proved to be. It certainly taught me the importance of 'just doing something'. It wasn't in my rock star schema for a band member to tune up halfway through a song. It happened and I did nothing. However, I did modify my schema and the next time I vowed I would do something. I figured anything was better than just standing there.

So in later gigs when the engineer forgot to turn the volume up for our opening, I adapted the Genesis creation myth ('let there be keyboards') and talked the instruments in, one by one. Everyone thought it was part of the show (apart from the awful sound). Later, at another gig, when the power went down except for the microphone, I did what anyone would have done in a dark basement on a scorching July evening. I began whistling 'Singing in the Rain'. The audience just joined in. Some even got there lighters out and swayed to and fro. Now that was in my rock star schema!

I never dreamed that any of these experiences would ever be useful again until I started lecturing. I worked at a place where the security policy seemed to be to lock everything up or leave everything open. Many times I started the lecture in the hallway. In fact, it seemed like only the burglars could get into the building. On top of that, if equipment can go wrong it will go wrong. Projector bulbs fail, video machines chew up tapes, DVDs stick, equipment sometimes doesn't arrive on time, the computer will crash, and on it goes. In most cases, doing anything is better than nothing at all. Better still, it pays to have a plan B.

I could have viewed each of these incidents as failures but instead I transformed them into feedback to create my 'show must go on' schema.

We all have past experiences containing transferable skills tucked away in old dusty schemas. If we take stock and polish them up, they may serve us well into the future. So what's in your 'show must go on' schema? Spend a few moments and jot down three incidents where your quick thinking got you out of a tight situation. Or, think of times when your persistence or ingenuity won the day.

Problem/incident	How you overcame it

Regularly updating this list can help to keep your transferable skills schema fresh and relevant. This means that when faced with a problem, you have greater confidence that you will be able to handle it. After all, if you've done it once, you can do it again. Essentially, it's about modelling your own past successes. After this brief look at the psychology of learning there is one final piece in the learning puzzle, that is, *persistence*.

THE VIRTUE OF PERSISTENCE

Persistence makes the learning cycle go round. Without it we would never learn anything. However, we need to model the persistence of the baby rather than the fly. The diagram below shows a model for our personal development. Again it's a cycle. We can move around it either way. Actions affect results, just as feedback affects future actions. Self-image affects our behaviour just as actions affect our self-image, and so on. Feedback affects our attitudes which in turn affect our potential and vice versa. Use this diagram as a reminder when faced with obstacles. Standing still is not an option!

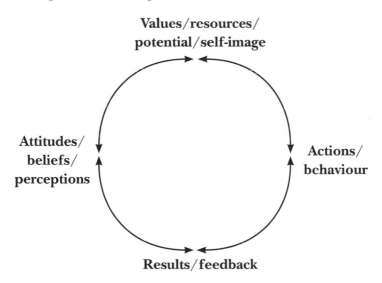

Values/resources/ potential/self-image

Attitudes/ beliefs/ perceptions

Actions/ behaviour

Results/feedback

Inevitably we will stumble and experience setbacks, and sometimes it will hurt. However, obstacles aren't end points, they are stopping-off points. They provide a pause for thought, which means fresh input for our schemas and filters. In many ways we need to be like a heat-seeking missile and lock on to our target. If it encounters obstacles, the missile does not storm off home feeling dejected. Being programmed for persistence, it uses the feedback, adjusts the coordinates and tries again and again, for as long as it takes.

Information is rather like a form of fuel that drives our lives. If we put higher quality fuel into an engine we improve the performance. In turn this improvement becomes the new fuel – the 'better information' that is fed back into the engine to produce further-enhanced performance. We ask better questions and we get better answers and on it goes.

Philosophers Ovid and Lucretius both pointed out that persistently dripping water will hollow stones. More than water, you have the power of insight, the ability to react to feedback, and to apply it.

DRYING OFF

Review: In this chapter we have pondered the learning cycle, its various stages and how this fits in with the principles of *insight, ownership* and *action*. Working with the learning cycle when we encounter setbacks we are able to treat them as feedback rather than failure. We have also considered the basic building blocks of learning (conditioning and modelling) and their impact on how we store knowledge about the world (schemas). The chapter has also highlighted the value of appropriate use of persistence in our lifelong learning.

In the next chapter we will consider the impact of our values and attitudes and their impact on our personal development and learning.

REFLECTION (*REFL-ACTION*)

1 **INSIGHT** (*Don't wait*): What are the three most important things you learned in this chapter?

(i)

(ii)

(iii)

2 **OWNERSHIP** (*It's your ship*): What impact has this had in terms of the way you think about your accountability for your life and goals?

3 **ACTION** (*Swim out to meet it*): What action will you take (*don't wait*) to make a positive change in your life? What personal experiment might you conduct to get feedback and insight?

Chapter Three

DUCKING AND DIVING

You are what you value

There was just enough heat to enhance the value of the breeze, and just enough wind to keep the whole sea in motion, to make the waves come bounding to the shore, foaming and sparkling, as if wild with glee.

Anne Brontë

If the wind will not serve, take to the oars.

Latin proverb

DIPPING A TOE

Preview: In this chapter we'll ponder the concepts of attitudes and values and their effects on our lives. We also look at the idea of matching values and goals and the implications on our personal development.

THE EBB AND FLOW OF IT

Bubbling under the surface, informing our choices and the direction of our lives, are our values. They are often out of sight but never really out of mind. They are our hidden motivators. They underpin the decisions and choices we make and the direction we take. The philosopher Ayn Rand went so far as to say that happiness comes from achieving our values.

Sometimes we decide to go with the flow and sometimes we swim against the tide. Sometimes we have a vague sense that this 'isn't me' or this is 'just right for me'. Sometimes we are confronted with something that offends all we stand for. Our values are like the tides of the ocean, the stars that guide our way, the sails and the oars all rolled into one!

Many of us share the same values – such as justice and freedom. To varying degrees we may uphold the values of truth, honour, fairness and loyalty. However, it is individual evaluations – our attitudes – that have us ducking and diving between choices. Working together, our attitudes and values create the ebb and flow which shapes our life's journeys and helps determine the destinations we reach. Cultural and individual values and attitudes are part of our perceptual filters (see Chapter One). They make up our individual map of the world. They determine our readiness to take action. So, before we continue, consider for a moment these questions, and note the answers in your journal.

- What do you value in your life?
- What do you stand for?
- What would you die for?
- What do you live for?

In this chapter, we'll consider the subject of values and attitudes as our own internal navigation system for personal development and positive outcomes. So, let's begin by looking at the subject of attitudes and how they contribute to your map of the world.

YOUR MAP OF THE WORLD
Fit and ready for action?
Have you been stopped in the street by someone with a clipboard eager to take 'just a few minutes of your time'? Have you ever been relaxing in the bath when the phone rings? You rush downstairs only to find it's someone who wants you to do a survey about products, services or behaviours. Halfway through a meal there's someone at the door with a badge and a clipboard. Television and magazine polls encourage us to call premium rate lines for the privilege of letting others know our attitudes. It seems it's not just money that makes the world go round; attitudes do too.

We all have attitudes and express them in the words we use and the choices we make, and seem to spend inordinate amounts of time telling people with clipboards about them! So, what constitutes an attitude and what function do attitudes serve? Let's consider these two questions in turn.

Components of an attitude
At the most basic level, an attitude is a feeling or evaluation towards something – that is, our likes and dislikes. So, we can have an attitude towards just about everything, from food, to people, to situations, and even our own values.

If we look at the Latin origin of the word attitude it means 'fit and ready for action'. So, attitudes create a mental state of readiness. Just like athletes on the starting line they provide the 'get ready, get steady' before the 'go'. However, although they prime us ready for action, it doesn't mean that we will always 'go'. Attitudes don't necessarily lead to particular behaviours; they just set up the mindset to make particular behaviours more likely. So, for instance, you may have the attitude that going to the gym and eating healthily are good for you but that doesn't automatically mean that you'll do either of them. It's rather like the guiding principles in this book. We can gain the insight and take ownership but not necessarily follow through on the action. Attitudes are general feelings, thoughts and evaluations – including our beliefs – which signal a *behavioural tendency*.

So, if attitudes cannot get us to go the gym or even get us out of bed in the morning, what function do they serve?

The function of attitudes

Out attitudes are filters that help us make sense of the world. They help us determine what we need to pay attention to and what we can ignore. According to psychologist Elliot Katz, attitudes serve four main functions. These are:

(i)   *The 'Good or Bad' function.* At the most basic level they are our likes and dislikes. Attitudes are evaluations of whether our feelings towards something are good or bad, positive or negative, useful or useless. By making this judgement, our attitudes help us to maximize the probability of having positive experiences while minimizing negative ones. Essentially, they draw us to the good stuff and away from the bad stuff.

(ii) *The 'How Does This Fit In' function.* Attitudes provide a framework to help us organize our perceptions and beliefs and to size up an event, object or person. Without attitudes every new situation would have to be approached from scratch. They help give us stability and consistency of meaning in the real world. Personal experience helps shape our attitudes but we inherit a host of ready-made ones in the form of the cultural norm, as we discussed in Chapter One. This means that sometimes we jump the gun, or rather jump to premature conclusions (prejudge), without waiting for the information. Each of us differs in the degree to which we need structure in our lives. This means that some people are more flexible in their approach to life, whereas others need the comfort of hard and fast, black and white categories. We will discuss this in greater depth in Chapter Nine.

(iii) *The 'Self-Defence' function.* At this level, attitudes often help us to deal with inner psychological problems and protect us from disturbing self-knowledge. Rather than face up to this knowledge we deny it, repress it or project it onto others, including our own faults. That's why people who never stop talking are forever complaining about people who never listen!

(iv) *The 'I Am What I Am' function.* Attitudes are a central part of our self-concept, our personal sense of identity. Our attitudes often make a statement about who we are, or rather who we think we are. Our identity is in part comprised of the things with which we identify. Attitudes are the means by which we communicate our values and provide an insight as to what is bubbling away under the surface.

The tests, exercises and quizzes in this book are tools to measure attitudes (and your tendency to take action), and in this chapter a means to uncover your system of values, that is, what drives you forward or holds you back.

YOUR SYSTEM OF VALUES
Do your values define you?

Almost every contestant in a beauty contest has probably at some time said 'I want to bring peace to the world'. As laudable as this seems, there are clearly other ways of bringing peace to the world that don't involve lip-gloss, high heels and a swimsuit. Although, wouldn't it be great if that was all it took? The value of 'bringing peace' in this context is more to do with the expectations that a contestant should be more than 'just a pretty face'.

What we value determines what we focus on and says something about who we are. Essentially, we are what we value. Our attitudes, together with our values, provide direction for behaviour and goals. Our system of values drives our attitudes, and influences the form that these attitudes take. It provides our individual and collective standards for evaluating actions, justifying opinions, conducting and planning behaviour, for deciding between different alternatives, engaging in social influence and presenting ourself to others. Of course, value systems vary between individuals, groups and different cultures.

Social psychologist Milton Rokeach makes explicit the connection between values and goals. He refers to values as *preferred end-states.* So, everything leads back to our values. And what else are goals if not preferred end-states or preferred outcomes? Essentially, goals are values in action!
There are broadly two types of values to consider:

(i) Instrumental values
(ii) Terminal values

Instrumental values
If we think in terms of a journey, instrumental values are the things that help us get from A to B. They are ports of call rather than the journey's end. For instance, ambition is a good example of an instrumental value. It isn't an end in itself but a means to an end. So, having ambition leads to success. Success is the endpoint and is what is known as a terminal value.

Terminal values
Terminal values are about the big issues in life and have a significant impact in determining and shaping our attitudes and also our goals. Terminal means 'end point': the journey's end. So, things like *equality* and *freedom* (and *success*) are examples of terminal values.
     As our values are the driving force in our life, matching goals to values helps to propel us forward to succeed, however we personally choose to define success.

Values: ebb and flow

The phrase 'value system' tells us that each of the values we hold do not work in isolation. They relate to one another, sometimes working with and sometimes against each other. We have a sense of the values we consider it desirable to move towards (approach values) and those which we prefer to move away from (avoidance values). For instance, we may value freedom and security in equal measure. If these clash, then we may have to chose one over the other. So, with our value system there is a pecking order. Some values are prized more highly than others. Insights and ownership of our individual value systems are crucial for getting to grips with what drives us – that is what motivates us to take action, or sometimes leads us to shy away from rocking the boat. In the following values assessment exercises, we'll consider both 'move towards' and 'move away from' values.

Values assessment

Do you know where you're going to?

In the first part of this assessment, consider what is important to move towards in your life – that is, the qualities and conditions you wish to embrace.

Circle any words or phrases that are particularly important to you or qualities you value in yourself or your life. It's not an exhaustive list so feel free to add your own.

The approach values list

excellence	passion	novelty	learning	equality
originality	liveliness	pleasure	common sense	being streetwise
assertiveness	courage	meaning	hard-work	security

carefulness	playfulness	modesty	genuineness	honesty
humanity	relaxation	ethics	generosity	teamwork
fairness	leadership	justice	self-control	inspiration
wealth	status	imagination	achievement	tradition
integrity	facts & figures	energy	communication	gratitude
spirituality	respect	faith	religiousness	forgiveness
optimism	bravery	fun & humour	individuality	curiosity
empathy	happiness	mercy	competition	cooperation
expertise	ingenuity	power	excitement	adventure
intimacy	sexiness	pride	perseverance	sincerity
service	community	peace	supportiveness	goodness
friendship	authority	enthusiasm	kindness	compassion
being liked	humility	uniqueness	tolerance	attachment
luxury	connectivity	love	sociability	altruism
tenderness	toughness	hope	appearance	transcendence
comfort	glamour	fashion	perfection	interaction
influence	significance	family	ambition	goal-orientation
romance	sensuality	esteem	independence	wisdom
discipline	success	health	contribution	belonging
certainty	youthfulness	fame	logic	intuition
professionalism	being right	objectivity	subjectivity	being needed
sense of purpose	open-mindedness	value for money	making a difference	appreciating beauty

Order of values

Now pause for a while and review and reflect on all the words and phrases you have circled. What do you notice? Are there any patterns? Pause for a moment to consider your choice of values.

1 Choose up to ten words or phrases that have the highest priority for you in terms of what you value.
2 Put these in column A. You may group together similar words if you wish.
3 After you have completed column A, you may wish to have a go at reordering your values using the process detailed below and put the new list in column B.

Column A: Your values list	Column B: to reorder values – see below
1	
2	
3	
4	
5	
6	
7	
8	
9	
10	

Reordering 'comparison process' (for column B)
You may already have a good idea which values are most important to you in your life. However, the following comparison process is a systematic method for ordering your values. It also helps to show the relative importance to you, as some values receive more points than others. An alternative method is simply to write each of your ten values on ten slips of paper. Move them around until you are happy with the order. The following method gives far richer feedback, however, and so is worth the extra bit of effort.

Follow these steps:

1 Begin with the value currently at the top of your list. Then compare it to every word that follows in your list.
2 Start by comparing 1st and 2nd values, then 1st and 3rd, the 1st and 4th and so on until you reach the end of the list.
3 For each comparison, decide which one of the pair is more important to you. Give that item one point.
4 Repeat this process down the list, each time giving one point to the most important value.
5 When you have compared the first item in the list with all the rest, move on to the second value in your list and repeat the process. So, now you are comparing 2nd with 3rd, 2nd with 4th, 2nd with 5th, and so on down the list.
6 Each time you make a comparison, award one point to the value in the pair that is most important to you.
7 Move on to the 3rd item in the list and repeat the process.
8 Continue until you are just comparing the two items at the bottom of your list.

9 Now add up all the points.

10 If you have any tied scores, do the same comparison process and give one point to the value that is more important to you.

11 Now put the words in order based on their points. The value with the highest score goes to the top. Write all the values in column B.

These are the values that act as *positive reinforcement* (see Chapter Two) for you. In other words, they are your preferred positive outcomes. You are motivated to take action to satisfy these values. We will discuss the concept of goal setting in Chapter Six.

Considering your list of values, what are your immediate thoughts? How does the reordered list differ from your first attempt? Are there are any surprises? How are your values determining your choices?

Before we move on to consider the 'avoidance' values, let's consider another personal development experiment.

Personal values experiment
Begin by rating the extent to which your actions support your values, on a scale from zero to ten. A score of zero means 'not at all' and a score of ten means 'totally'. You are free to use any point along the scale.

Extent to which actions support values

0	1	2	3	4	5	6	7	8	9	10
not at all					moderately					totally

To help explore opportunities and possibilities, ask yourself the following questions:

1   What is it that has helped me to get from zero to where I am now?

2   What is it that tells me that I'm at that point on the scale and not at zero?

3   What things can I imagine doing when I am one point higher along the scale? What else? List them:

(i)

(ii)

(iii)

(iv)

(v)

4   What one thing will I try out to see if it will make a difference to my rating for taking action on my values?

Repeat this for your second and third highest values. This will give you three actions you are prepared to carry out to support your values. I could try:

1

2

3

Now pick one of these things and take action on it. After you have completed it, repeat the zero to ten scaling.

Extent to which actions support values

0	1	2	3	4	5	6	7	8	9	10
not at all					moderately					totally

Did you action move your rating higher up the scale? If not, why do you think that is? What adjustments could you make? What else could you try? Now come the big questions:

1   What will represent 'good enough' for you? What number on the scale? How will you know when you get there? What will you be doing differently to what you're doing now?
2   How will you know when you're at ten?

This process is incredibly effective for personal development. It helps to quantify progress and the questions are designed to generate good feedback. The questions also help to generate goals, which will turn into compelling action plans in Chapter Six.

In the meantime, let's return to the proposition that living to our values increases happiness with another little personal experiment.

Personal happiness experiment
Now ask yourself: If I was routinely meeting my values what impact would that have on my happiness? Let's go one step further and translate this into action with another personal experiment.

• Before you begin, rate your happiness on a scale from zero to ten. Where zero equals totally unhappy and ten equals totally happy. You can use any number along the scale to reflect how you feel.

Happiness rating

0	1	2	3	4	5	6	7	8	9	10
not at all			moderately							totally

- Now go back to your top three values and decide on further actions you could try out to support your values.
- After a week or a month, repeat the zero to ten rating. What impact did your value-matched actions have on your happiness?
- What is it that has helped you to get from zero to where you are now?
- What is it that tells you that you're at that point on the scale and not at zero?
- What will represent good enough for you on your happiness rating? How will you know when you get there?
- What do you imagine doing that will make it a ten?

Again, this feedback will be useful for your goal setting (Chapter Six).

(By the way, how's the personal experiment in 'gratitude and anticipation' going, from Chapter One?)

Now that you have a clearer idea of what you want to move towards with your approach values, let's consider things that you want to move away from – your avoidance values.

Avoidance values: da doo run run

The instructions are the same as for the previous exercise, except that you are now focusing on your avoidance values; the things you want to move away from. You're in a powerboat, hightailing it out of there! Circle any word or phrase that is particularly important for you to move away from or avoid in your life. Add your own if you wish.

The avoidance values list

failure	unhappiness	depression	anxiety	worry
lack of choices	abandonment	poverty	debt	rejection
anger	frustration	fear	humiliation	guilt
stress	powerlessness	bitterness	procrastination	insecurity
envy	moaning	promiscuity	gossiping	making excuses
jealousy	hatred	prejudice	disapproval	disappointment
boredom	conflict	selfishness	feeling inadequate	helplessness
incompetence	weakness	laziness	low self-esteem	lack of confidence
self-doubt	losing	being ignored	feeling belittled	ineffectualness
negativity	ill-health	overweight	underweight	being unfit
taken for granted	chaos	untidiness	embarrassment	loneliness
grief	danger	indifference	coldness	aloofness
greed	revenge	ignorance	being unpopular	rudeness
disrespect	cruelty	dullness	intolerance	apathy
tiredness	isolation	ugliness	emptiness	cowardice
tactlessness	hurt	obligation	being a doormat	hopelessness
confrontation	persecution	obsession	addiction	spitefulness
aggression	aimlessness	pointlessness	disorder	bloody-mindedness
problems	dishonesty	immorality	fear of death	unassertive
sinfulness	ungodliness	impurity	lack of passion	alienation
pain	feeling unloved	discrimination	amateurism	feeling unwanted
unforgiving	loss of dignity	frailty	redundancy	irresponsible
uselessness	being disliked	blandness	not being heard	feeling invisible
victimization	confusion	feeling undermined	feeling misunderstood	feeling out of control

Order of values

Pause for a moment to consider your list of chosen values before continuing.

- Choose the ten words or phrases that have the highest priority for you in terms of what you want to avoid or move away from in your life. Put these in column A. As before, you may group together similar words if you wish.
- After you have completed column A, try reordering your values using the process detailed below and put the new list in column B.

Column A: Your values list	Column B: to reorder values – see below
1	
2	
3	
4	
5	
6	
7	
8	
9	
10	

You may already have a good idea which values are most important for you to move away from in your life. Remember this time you are awarding points to the value you want to move away from. However, as you follow the comparison process it is the *worst* value that gets the point each time.

Follow these steps:

1 As before, begin with the value currently at the top of your list. You will then compare it to every word that follows in your list.

2 Start by comparing 1st and 2nd values, then 1st and 3rd, 1st and 4th, 1st and 5th and so on until you reach the end of the list.

3 For each comparison, decide which one of the pair is more important for you to move away from. Remember the worst value gets the point.

4 Repeat this process all the way down the list, each time giving one point to the value you most want to move away from.

5 When you have compared the first item in the list with all the rest, move on to the second value in your list and repeat the process. So, now you are comparing 2nd with 3rd, 2nd with 4th, 2nd with 5th, 2nd with 6th and so on all the way down the list.

6 Each time you make a comparison, award one point to the value in the pair that is most important for you to move away from.

7 Move on to the third item in the list and repeat the process.

8 Continue until you are just comparing the two items at the bottom of your list.

9 Now add up all the points.

10 If you have any tied scores, do the same comparison process and give one point to the value that it is most important you move away from (that is, the worst one of the two).

11 Now put the words in order based on their points. The highest score goes at the top. Write the values in column B.

These are the values that act as *negative reinforcement* (see Chapter Two) for you. You are motivated to act to remove these things from your life or else to remove yourself from what you perceive causes them. We will discuss coping strategies in Chapter Nine (overcoming self-sabotage). However, for the moment consider two possible courses of action. You can root out these negative reinforcers at their source and take control of the situation (fight). Alternatively, you can just get the hell out of there (flight). We'll discuss this concept in greater depth in Chapter Five (relaxation). In the meantime let's tie up the loose ends and turn the tables on those avoidance values.

A reversal of fortune

You now have your list of ten values in your life that you wish to move away from. So what are you going to do, spend your life running from them? Wouldn't it be better if you could take this insight, own it, and turn it into something positive? You can.

Exercise

Write out the top ten avoidance values again and beside each one write its exact opposite. For instance if you have put 'anxiety and stress' in first place, then write 'relaxation' opposite.

	Things to avoid	Opposite
1		
2		
3		
4		
5		
6		
7		
8		
9		
10		

You have now converted your top avoidance values into approach values. You may even notice some overlap with your approach values list.

Finding the opposite of what we want to avoid creates more opportunities to find things we want to move towards, to achieve more positive outcomes. So, if you feel anxious and stressed, what small steps can you make this month, this week or today to move you towards your goal of relaxation?

Choose your top three converted 'opposites' and repeat the personal experiments and scaling questions for happiness.

Ideals like stars

Mohandas Gandhi argued that our values are our destiny. Setting goals without matching them to your values is like sailing at night with no instrument panel and no stars. You'll end up somewhere but it may well be a question of fate rather than an answer to your preferred end-state. Carl Rogers stated that we always move in a positive direction given the necessary and sufficient conditions to do so. Matching goals to values provides a crucial condition for getting us primed and ready for action to chart the course of our lives.

DRYING OFF

Review: In this chapter we pondered the effects our attitudes and values have on our view of the world and how we relate to it. Our filters include our values and attitudes. What we want from life is determined by how we relate to the world and how we perceive ourselves as agents in it. We have considered both approach and avoidance values and how these act as motivational reinforcement. Finally we have contemplated the importance of matching values and goals to achieve positive outcomes and our preferred end-states.

There are many more opportunities to explore your values and attitudes throughout this book. In the next chapter, we are going to focus on the related subject of playing to your strengths.

REFLECTION (*REFL-ACTION*)

1   **INSIGHT**: What are the three most important things you learned in this chapter?

(i)

(ii)

(iii)

2   **OWNERSHIP**: What impact has this had in terms of the way you think about your accountability for your life and goals?

3   **ACTION**: What action does this inspire you to take to make a positive change in your life and move closer to your preferred end-states? What personal experiment might you conduct to get feedback and insight?

Chapter Four

SOS!

Support our strengths

Talent develops in tranquillity, character in the full current of human life.

Johann Wolfgang von Goethe

Look well into thyself; there is a source of strength which will always spring up if thou wilt always look there.

Marcus Aurelius Antoninus

Water its living strength first shows, when obstacles its course oppose.

Johann Wolfgang von Goethe

DIPPING A TOE
Preview: In this chapter we'll ponder the benefits of playing to our strengths, in particular looking at individual learning styles and also examing the links between strengths and happiness.

MUST TRY HARDER – COULD DO BETTER

We've all probably heard the phrases 'must try harder' or 'could do better' at some time in our lives. Maybe they have been directed at you. Throughout our lives, in learning and development, the emphasis is more often on overcoming weaknesses. Playing to our strengths frequently takes a back seat. So, what do you think might happen if we switched the emphasis? Well, throughout this book, we are doing just that, particularly in this chapter. We move towards a strengths-focused approach (and move away from a weakness-centred one). In effect, we concentrate on making the most of what we have, not hankering for what we don't have.

We further develop this approach to include personal learning styles, building on what we know about the learning cycle (Chapter Two) and considering the topic of personal learning styles.

HOW DID YOU DO THAT?

To get a better idea of what we are moving away from, imagine a child arriving home with 96% on a science test. Jubilantly, the child bursts through the front door, waving her test paper, eager to show it to her parents. We might expect the child to be met with 'Well done', 'That's amazing, I'm really proud of you', or 'That's incredible, how did you do that?' These are all appropriate responses to such an impressive result. Instead, try 'What happened to the other 4%?' In effect, jubilation turns to dismay and 96% actually becomes a failure!

The sad thing is that this is often a routine response. We focus on the failure and overshadow the success. There isn't a word to describe 96% in the marking scheme; it's something beyond excellence. Yet if we focus on the missing 4%, it's as if we need not have bothered at all. From a strengths-based approach however, we first take stock of what we have achieved. It doesn't matter if it's 30% or 40%. Let's look at how we got there, before looking at how we can move on. We would not say to a baby after it took its first step: 'How come you didn't run round the dining table?' Instead, we would focus on what it did right and build upon it! That's how we all learn. By reflecting on how we've achieved a result we reinforce our learning by strengthening the associations between insight, action and success.

So, here are some strengths-building questions to help you focus on what you have already attained, whether it be 96%, 57% or 22%. First focus on what you've got by asking:

- What did you do to get that result?
- Was there anything that you think really helped that you can do more of?
- What strengths or qualities helped you get this far?
- What did you do differently this time?
- Is there something that you used to do that you stopped doing this time?
- What can you let go of that didn't help?
- What else did you do?

Take a moment to write the answers in your journal. These questions are designed to elicit the success strategy of *insight, ownership* and *action*. What often emerges is that just a few key things contributed to the result. This is known as the *Pareto Principle*. It has been observed, over and over again, that 20% of what you do contributes to 80% of the result. The above questions will help uncover the all-important 20%. In effect, you get to work smarter not harder. Remember the fly from Chapter Two? It beat its head against 80% of the closed window, when all it had to do was focus on the 20% that was open!

In Chapter Two we considered the learning cycle with the four phases of the learning process: *action, reflection, theory* and *practice.* Well, each of us has a particular preference for where we start in the cycle of learning. Some of us dive right in, some sit back and reflect, some start with a theory and yet others focus on practicalities. Where we start in the learning cycle colours our learning style and the way we approach problems. Whatever insights we have in this regard can help us play to our strengths.

PREFERRED PERSONAL LEARNING STYLES

Each of us has a tendency to enter the learning cycle at a preferred point. There's no wrong or right, just different. These inclinations indicate our preferred personal learning styles.

As you read through the following descriptions you may recognize something of yourself in each of the categories. They are based on the work of Peter Honey and Alan Mumford and, for the purposes of this book, I have simplified the terminology. As you read through the descriptions just make a note of which ones most closely describe you.

Active style

'They that hesitate are lost'

People with an active learning style are characterized by an enthusiastic, 'here and now', act-first-think-later approach. Day-to-day routine tasks and long explanations may bore people with an active style. Instead they enjoy novel experiences and being thrown in at the deep end. People with this style are unlikely to read manuals because they prefer to work it out for themselves. They are more likely to be the first people to contribute at meetings but may jump to premature conclusions. They enjoy role-playing and being the centre of attention. They are often the life and soul of the party.

Reflective style

'Look before you leap'

Characteristically, people with a reflective learning style adopt a more cautious, stand-back-and-weigh-up-the-options approach. Such people tend to take a back seat and are somewhat slower in offering opinions or reaching conclusions. They learn best when they can observe and review, prepare and get an idea of the big picture. Typically they don't like taking the lead or role-playing. They dislike being rushed, are worried by tight deadlines or being thrown in at the deep end.

Theorizing Style

'Does it make sense?'

A theorizing style is marked by a tendency to think problems through in a logical manner. People with this style often take a rational and objective approach and try fitting facts and assumptions into sound theories. Typically they take a logical, structured, step-by-step approach to problem solving. They tend to ask questions rather than make statements with a view to uncovering underlying principles. They do not work so well in situations that emphasize emotions and feelings. Instead, they work best when they are well briefed – preferring structure and clear objectives.

Practical style

'Does it work?'

People with a practical style typically enjoy considering new ideas and experimenting. They are keen to find out the practical applications of theories and techniques. They tend to act quickly and confidently and prefer to get straight to the point. Characteristically, people with this style quickly become impatient with endless discussion. They are hands-on and down-to-earth, with a tendency to learn best when there is an obvious link between theory and task. They enjoy role-playing. People with this style tend not to learn so well in 'all theory' situations or without practical guidelines.

Determining your own learning style

Simply reading through the descriptions above will give you an idea of your preferred learning styles. You'll probably find that you're drawn to one description from the action–reflection pair and one from the theory–practice pair (see scale below). Placing a tick in the end boxes constitutes a strong preference for a particular style, whereas towards the middle represents more of a mixture.

Action	· · ·	· · ·	· · ·	· · ·	· · ·	· · ·	Reflection
	strong	*moderate*	*slight*	*slight*	*moderate*	*strong*	
Theory	· · ·	· · ·	· · ·	· · ·	· · ·	· · ·	Practice

Place the tick in the box not on the line. Each of the boxes has three dots to allow you to indicate a sense of strength of style above the basic strong, moderate and slight categories. There are no right or wrong answers. This feedback is for you alone to use. So, simply indicate the styles to which you are most drawn and we'll use the feedback in another personal experiment. However, before we continue, I'd just like to point out that you can gain further insights by checking out the comprehensive questionnaire devised by Peter Honey and Alan Mumford (see Further Reading).

Personal experiment
Rating yourself highly on one dimension in the pair (action–reflection and theory–practice) means you are more likely to be comfortable in that type of learning environment (and less comfortable in the other). The aim of this experiment is to gain more insight (feedback) by doing things out of your comfort zone.

For your two strongest preference styles look at the following sections and try out one of the suggestions for one week.

Suggestions for active style
Try one of these for a week:

- Practise people-watching simply by observing other people's behaviour;
- Keep a diary or a journal (or at least complete the reflection section at the end of each chapter);
- Practice drawing up the pros and cons of a particular course of action, in effect, looking before you leap.

Suggestions for reflective style
Try one of these for a week:

- Try doing something new during this week;
- Practise initiating small talk with strangers;

- Break up the day into a range of activities (doing rather than just reflecting), including practising thinking on your feet.

Suggestions for theorizing style
Try one of these for a week:

- Concentrate on producing action plans (setting goals);
- Collect some practical techniques and experiment with them;
- Tackle a DIY project or construct an item of flat-pack furniture.

Suggestions for practical style
Try one of these for a week:

- Read something that is 'heavy', theoretical and thought-provoking;
- Practise spotting inconsistencies in arguments and ask probing questions designed to get to the crux of the matter;
- Consider a complex task, conduct an in-depth analysis of it and look for underlying principles.

At the end of the week consider the feedback this personal experiment has given you:

- How did you feel?
- What insights did you gain?

There will be many occasions when situations are not optimal for your personal preferred learning style. When you become aware that there is a mismatch, you have a choice: you can either endure it with insight or make a small change to accommodate it.

However, this is only part of the picture; as you become more aware of your learning styles and preferences, a greater range of choices and options open up for you.

In Chapter Two we considered how we process information. This leads us to the subject of our five senses.

MAKING SENSE

We take in information via our five senses: vision, hearing, touch, taste and smell. Although sight and hearing are ordinarily the dominant two senses, different people have varying degrees of preference for which sense they favour when learning. The main three sense preferences are:

- *Visual preference* (sight)
- *Audio preference* (hearing)
- *Kinaesthetic (tactile) preference* (touch)

To give you some simple examples, we might expect a painter to have a strong visual preference, a musician might have a strong audio preference and a sculptor a stronger kinaesthetic preference, although inevitably there will be a crossover. Here's a brief test to help you assess your sense preference.

Sense preference quiz
There are no right or wrong answers, so just respond in a way that you feel most accurately reflects you.

Instructions
- For each of the questions you have five points to share out between the three options (a, b and c).

- To indicate that something is a lot like you, give it more points. If it's only a little like you, give it fewer points. If it's nothing like you, don't give it any points.
- It's up to you how you share out the points for each question, as long as they add up to five. For example: 5,0,0; 2,1,2; or 1,0,4 – or any other combination.
- The only restriction is that you should not use fractions.

The quiz

1 To relax would you prefer to:
  (a)_____ Watch television or a DVD?
  (b)_____ Listen to music?
  (c)_____ Do something active, like going to the gym or for a walk?
2 If you need to spell a word do you:
  (a)_____ Picture the word in your head?
  (b)_____ Break it down into component sounds, saying it out loud?
  (c)_____ Write it down and see if it feels right?
3 When you read, do you prefer:
  (a)_____ Descriptive scenes?
  (b)_____ Lots of dialogue?
  (c)_____ Action stories (or not a keen reader)?
4 When talking would you be more likely to use the expression:
  (a)_____ I see what you mean?
  (b)_____ I hear what you're saying?
  (c)_____ I'm getting a feel for this?
5 When you are trying to concentrate, what would be most likely distract you?
  (a)_____ Movement or untidiness.

(b) _____ Sounds or noises.

(c) _____ Activity going on around you, or changes in temperature.

6 When you meet people again after a long time are you more likely to:

(a) _____ Forget their names but remember their faces or where you met?

(b) _____ Remember the name and what you talked about before you 'place the face'?

(c) _____ Remember best the activity you did together?

7 When you have to contact people on business do you:

(a) _____ Prefer to deal face-to-face?

(b) _____ Prefer the telephone?

(c) _____ Prefer to 'do lunch' or talk over an activity?

8 When you have to assemble something, do you prefer to:

(a) _____ Look at the pictures and directions in the manual?

(b) _____ Call a help desk or get someone to explain it to you?

(c) _____ Just try to figure it out as you go along?

Scoring instructions

Add up your responses.

- Total for (a): _____ is your VISUAL score.

- Total for (b): _____ is your AUDIO (verbal) score.

- Total for (c): _____ is your KINAESTHETIC (tactile) score.

SENSE PREFERENCE: WHAT IT MEANS

Looking through the items in the quiz you may have already gleaned an idea of the implications of the different learning styles. Scoring highly on any of the three senses indicates a preference for taking information in this way.

Highest score

If your highest score is *visual,* it indicates that you favour the sense of sight when learning and tend to prefer diagrams, pictures and maps, especially in lectures and presentations. You prefer to watch TV or film to relax and are more likely to enjoy descriptive books that evoke strong imagery. You always remember a face and prefer to look people in the eye when doing business. You are usually good at assembling the type of flat pack furniture that comes with instructions just in pictures.

If your highest score is *audio,* it indicates that you favour the sense of hearing when learning and tend to prefer verbal instructions. To relax you are more likely to listen to music and enjoy books with lots of dialogue. You tend to be better at remembering names, and like doing business over the telephone. When trying to assemble flat pack furniture you are more likely to call the help desk or call someone so they can talk you through it.

If your highest score is *kinaesthetic,* it indicates that you favour the sense of touch when learning and tend to prefer practical activities. To relax you prefer to do something active even if it's just going for a walk. You are most likely not a keen reader unless it's an action-based story. You tend to prefer to do business over lunch or engaged in an activity, and are much more likely to remember people on the basis of what you did together. When assembling flat pack furniture, you are more likely to get stuck in and try it out as you go along on the basis of what feels right.

So what if my scores are pretty much the same?

If your scores are roughly the same it indicates that you have no strong sense preference and use all equally or as the situation demands it. However, it is important to point out that the quiz is only an approximation of your sense preference. It's not meant to be a label you attach to yourself. Rather, it is another bit of insight that may help you identify when situations are not geared to your ideal learning conditions. This may be enough to help you tolerate the situation. However, you may wish to set yourself more of a challenge and experiment with doing things outside your comfort zone. To do this, go back to the questions and try out some of your less preferred options over the next week or so. This will help you explore the limits of your filtered view of the world. You may come back to the same strengths and that is fine, but you may uncover some hidden ones in the process. You won't know unless you experiment.

All the material we have covered so far in this chapter is about knowing your own strengths. If you wish to gain further insights into your learning style, then the Further Reading section in this book contains a list of resources. One recommended resource is the *Index of Learning Styles* devised by Barbara Soloman and Richard Felder, which combines learning styles and sense preferences.

KNOWING YOUR OWN STRENGTH

In recent years there has been a shift away from the traditional weakness-centred approach to personal development.

In his work on teambuilding, R. Meredith Belbin offers nine distinct team-role types, each comprising strengths and 'allowable weaknesses'. He advocates that weaknesses should be managed rather than corrected. Weaknesses are the other side of the coin to strengths and by correcting them we could end up compromising our strengths. In *Now, Discover Your Strengths*, Marcus Buckingham and Donald Clifton take a similar approach, offering 34 possible key strengths and, through a detailed assessment questionnaire, an individual's top five strengths are determined. According to their view, it does not make economic sense to focus on eradicating weaknesses. Instead we work on maximizing our strengths. As for our weaknesses, Buckingham and Clifton recommend that we get someone with a complementary pattern of strengths do things for us, but this is not always feasible. Alternatively, they propose that we just improve our weaknesses to a point where they are just 'good enough to get by'. We don't have to excel at everything!

In *Authentic Happiness*, Seligman argues that happiness can be found in playing to our strengths or rather in living them day by day. Looking back on the values exercise in the previous chapter, you may consider many of the things you value also to be your strong points. Often we value more highly and find joy in our strengths.

Overall, a strengths-focused approach makes sound psychological sense. Just as we can't process every tiny piece of information that comes our way (cognitive economy: Chapter One), nor can we be expected to be absolutely fabulous at absolutely everything! It is essential we are selective.

The following exercise represents a simplified strengths-finder exercise to provide a basis for exploring the strengths-based approach to personal development. It includes key terms from the authors mentioned above (most notably Seligman).

Strengths list

As in the values exercises in the previous chapter, circle any words or phrases that you consider to be your strengths. You may circle words that have similar meaning and group them together for the next stage in the exercise. You may also add your own strengths too.

Strengths list

action	reflection	theorizing	practicality
curiosity	interest in the world	love of learning	judgement
critical thinking	open-mindedness	ingenuity	originality
common sense	being street-wise	social competence	self-understanding
emotional awareness	perspective	courage	bravery
perseverance	hard working	diligence	integrity
honesty	genuineness	kindness	generosity
showing love	being loved	citizenship	duty
teamwork	loyalty	fairness	equity
leadership	self-control	carefulness	discretion
caution	humility	modesty	appreciation of beauty
excellence appreciation	gratitude	hope	optimism
goal-directedness	spirituality	sense of purpose	faith
religiousness	forgiveness	mercy	playfulness
humour	zest for life	excitement	enthusiasm

Order of strengths

Now pause for a while to review and reflect on all the words and phrases you have circled. What do you notice? Are there any patterns? So now:

1   Choose up to ten words or phrases that that you feel represent your main (key) strengths.
2   Put these in column A. You may group together similar words if you wish.
3   After you have completed column A, use the same process that you used to reorder you values in Chapter Three (you can also use the simple sort method using slips of paper).

Column A: Your strengths list	Column B: to reorder strengths – see Chapter Three
1	
2	
3	
4	
5	
6	
7	
8	
9	
10	

Personal experiment

So, to what extent do your actions support your top strengths? As before, rate this on a scale from zero to ten. A score of zero means 'not at all' and a score of ten means 'totally'. You are free to use any point along the scale.

Extent to which actions support strengths

0	1	2	3	4	5	6	7	8	9	10
not at all					moderately					totally

To help explore opportunities and possibilities, ask yourself the following questions:

1   What is it that has helped me to get from zero to where I am now?
2   What is it that tells me I'm at that point on the scale and not at zero?
3   What things can I imagine doing when I am one point higher along the scale? What else? List them:
    (i)

    (ii)

    (iii)

    (iv)

    (v)

4   What one thing will I try out to see if it would make a difference to my rating for taking action on my strengths?

Repeat this for your second and third highest values. This will give you three actions you are prepared to carry out to support your strengths.

I could try:

1

2

3

Now pick one of these things and take action on it. After you have completed it, repeat the zero to ten scaling.

Extent to which actions support strengths

0	1	2	3	4	5	6	7	8	9	10
not at all				moderately						totally

Did your action move your rating higher up the scale? If not, why do you think that is? What adjustments could you make? What else could you try? Now come the big questions:

1 What will represent 'good enough' for you? What number on the scale? How will you know when you get there? What will you be doing differently to what you're doing now?
2 How will you know when you're at ten?

In the previous chapter we considered the idea that living to your values increases happiness. So now let's consider Seligman's proposition that living to our strengths increases our happiness through another personal experiment.

Happiness and strengths experiment

Ask yourself: If I was routinely supporting my strengths what impact would that have on my happiness?

• Before you begin, rate your happiness on a scale from zero to ten where zero equals totally unhappy and ten equals totally happy. You can use any number along the scale to reflect how you feel.

Happiness rating

0	1	2	3	4	5	6	7	8	9	10
not at all					**moderately**					**totally**

Now go back to your top three strengths and decide on further actions you could try out to support them.

• After a week or a month, repeat the zero to ten rating. What impact did your strengths-focused actions have on your happiness?
• What is it that has helped you to get from zero to where you are now?
• What is it that tells you that you're at that point on the scale and not at zero?
• What will represent good enough for you on your happiness rating? How will you know when you get there?
• What do you imagine doing that will make it a ten?

Again, this feedback will be useful for your goal setting (Chapter Six). Deeper insights into our personal preferred learning styles and strengths help foster a stronger sense of ownership, offering a clearer picture of the actions we need to take to achieve positive lasting change.

In the next section, we consider the relationship between identity and change.

BUT THAT'S JUST THE WAY I AM

There's a big difference between 'I am what I am' and 'that's just the way I am', apart from the sequins! The former is about playing to strengths and the latter about pandering to weaknesses. Although many features of our personality appear stable, our values and goals shift, leading to subtle (and not so subtle) changes in our sense of identity. Before discussing the relationship between identity and change, let's consider a couple of factors that people often get hung up about.

Either/or

There are two concepts that crop up regularly in self-help books and media stories: gender differences and brain differences. I have deliberately avoided both of these topics for very good reasons. Firstly, the differences between the genders (male and female) are vastly overstated. Cutting-edge research helps to put it all into context: the similarities we share are far greater than our differences. Secondly, the phrases 'right brain' and 'left brain', although often used, are incorrect. Whenever you see these, you can be sure that the subject is being oversimplified. Yes, specific tasks require different areas of the brain. However, new research suggests there's much more of a crossover between the two sides of the brain. The nature of the task and the particular situation we find ourselves in are much more important. Furthermore, left brain/right brain divisions are often just thinly veiled gender stereotypes.

When we read stuff that seems to argue that our differences and limitations are enshrined in biology, it may discourage us from even trying. There are assertive, logical women in the world and nurturing, empathic men and a whole spectrum of difference in between. Our aim should not be to get in touch with our masculine or feminine sides but rather to become more rounded psychologically. The value underpinning this book is that our identity lies in our individual strengths and how we put them to the test, not in generalized stereotypes. Here ends this chapter's soapbox caveat!

Sense of identity
We arrive at our personal sense of identity from a number of different factors. Certainly our behaviour and the responses to our actions contribute to the sense of our personal strengths. Our attitudes and values determine our choices and say a great deal about who we are. Our environment and the situations in which we find ourselves may mediate all of these. NLP trainer Robert Dilts has argued that our sense of identity is subject to various levels of cognitive processing, a view that is supported by evidence-based psychology. We tend to think about identity as something that just is. However, our sense of identity is something we work to maintain in the face of challenges. It is also quite susceptible to change. It's helpful to think of the whole process as a chain reaction, or a chain of command:

The cognitive chain of command

If we have to work to maintain our sense of identity it also means that with the right input we can change it at will. For example, we can effect change to add qualities such as confidence, or delete behaviours that no longer serve us. It all hinges on two concepts, those of control and influence. Let's consider these in the context of the following diagram before considering practical examples of how the process works:

environment & situations   behaviour & thoughts   values & attitudes   skills & strengths   identity

Control

If we begin on the left-hand side we can see that different environments and situations exert control over our behaviour and thoughts. For instance, we behave very differently with our friends at a party than we would with our work colleagues in a meeting. In turn our thoughts and actions tend to control our values and attitudes.

Further along the chain, our values and attitudes control our strengths, which in turn control our identity. However, this process works both ways.

Influence

This time if we start from the right-hand side we can see that our sense of identity has an influence on our strengths and skills. Just think – the first step to acquiring any new skill is seeing yourself as a person who could gain that skill. As we work back along the chain, our strengths and skills in turn influence our values and attitudes. These in turn influence our behaviours and thoughts which may then exert an influence on particular environments and situations, and at the very least how we perceive those situations and environments.

Insight – Ownership – Action

Insight into the cognitive chain of command enables us to take ownership of our sense of identity and our ability to make changes (take action) in line with our personal preferred outcomes. Let's consider some examples of how this works in practice:

Smoking

Many programmes encourage people by working on their attitudes and mainly consider the health benefits. However, it may be more effective to go further long the chain to identity. If you start by seeing yourself as a non-smoker this has a knock-on effect in terms of attitudes and values which in turn have an impact on your thoughts and behaviours. As a non-smoker the thoughts are also directed to specific situations and the environment. So, if you make changes at the level of environment by avoiding psychological cues that trigger thoughts of smoking, this will affect your behaviour and, in turn, your values and attitudes, all the way back to identity.

Eating patterns

From a personal perspective I have in the past defined myself as a 'chocoholic' or a 'caffeine addict'. These labels did nothing to help my attempts at moderation. The identity label exerted a strong influence on my behaviour. In effect I defined myself in terms of my over consumption. When I became a person who loved chocolate and coffee, surprisingly my consumption lowered. I then took it a step further and introduced the word 'good'. I switched brands to higher quality varieties and found that they were more satisfying. I didn't crave the cheap and cheerful stuff so much. I then revisited my values and switched to Fairtrade and organic brands. As my local corner shop doesn't sell the Fairtrade organic chocolate brands, my change in values has wrought a change in my environment. I still enjoy chocolate a few times a week, but now I really savour the moment. In many ways it has become even more special. It's now a more rare but richer experience, almost a sacred one. The result is that I'm now a lot closer to my ideal weight.

This process can be used for any aspect of personal development such as increasing confidence.

Confidence

Confidence is not a natural-born quality but rather a learned behaviour or mindset. Levels of confidence vary depending on context. In different situations and environments we are more confident than in others. So, for someone who wishes to build confidence, a first step is to relax, then begin to recognize opportunities to practise confidence skills in favourable environments. If you can do it in one environment you can transfer these skills to another situation. In effect, you model your own behaviour. It's also a good idea to observe others and model the various behaviours that comprise confidence. These changes in behaviour can have a knock-on effect in terms of values, attitudes, skills and strengths. Of course, it helps if you can at least picture yourself behaving confidently. Imagining yourself as someone who is developing confidence can also have a knock-on effect along the chain right back to environment and situation. In time you may learn that you can influence situations and environments. As you engage in this multidimensional approach, your attitudes will change too, especially if you apply the feedback. In Chapters Seven and Eight we will consider developing new skills to work on our view of ourselves (identity).

As you can see from these examples it helps to view things in terms of constantly flexing boundaries rather than fixed states. We can push our boundaries and limitations. It doesn't require superhuman effort. It's just a case of redirecting our energies. After all, we work hard to keep these boundaries in place so it takes no more effort to test them. Rather than waiting for things to take shape, become the shaper. Our sense of identity is a part of our value system and as such determines our choices. In effect it can propel us forward or hold us back.

TAKE IT TO THE BRIDGE

A ship's bridge is the place where the navigational controls are housed and operated. The first section of this book has taken us from *insight* to *ownership,* in helping to take command of our own navigational controls. You're shipshape, seaworthy and ready to set sail. As Marcel Proust says: 'The real voyage of discovery consists not in seeking new landscapes but in having new eyes'. This section has been about rethinking perceptions and creating that new perspective in preparation for the next part of the voyage.

In the following section, the four chapters take us further on the journey from *ownership* to *action*. Relaxation, goal setting, visualization and self-talk form the basic psychological skills for peak performance and are used routinely in sports psychology. You'll learn to apply them to everyday life for positive lasting change.

DRYING OFF

Review: In this chapter, as well as exploring the links with the previous chapters in this section, we pondered the benefits of adopting a strengths-focused approach on personal development and learning, as opposed to the more weakness-based approach. Developing the themes of insight and ownership, we considered individual learning styles and sense preference.

In the next port of call we adopt an approach with a stronger emphasis on practical skills, informed by the insights from this section. We begin with the topic of relaxation.

REFLECTION (*REFL-ACTION*)

1 **INSIGHT**: What are the three most important things you learned in this chapter?

(i)

(ii)

(iii)

2 **OWNERSHIP**: What impact has this had in terms of the way you think about your accountability for your life and goals?

3 **ACTION**: What action does this inspire you to take to make a positive change in your life and move closer to your preferred end-states? What personal experiment might you conduct to get feedback and insight?

part two:

FROM
OWNERSHIP
TO ACTION

Chapter Five

LUCIDITY AND STILLNESS

The opposite of stress

> *If water derives lucidity from stillness, how much more the faculties of the mind! The mind of the sage, being in repose, becomes the mirror of the universe, the speculum of all creation.*
>
> Chuang Tzu
>
> *To the mind that is still, the whole universe surrenders.*
>
> Lao Tzu

DIPPING A TOE

Preview: In this chapter we'll ponder the psychology and physiology of stress and relaxation including the mind–body connection. We'll explore different breathing and meditation techniques to interrupt the stress cycle, and reflect on relaxation as the foundation of confidence.

THE OPPOSITE OF STRESS

In the hustle and bustle of modern life, relaxation can seem like a luxury. People protest that they don't have time or can't afford to relax. When we are under pressure or stressed, relaxation time is the first thing we sacrifice. All too often, relaxation is viewed as dispensable or a waste of time. This chapter ponders the opposite view. According to ancient Chinese philosophers, mental stillness and lucidity go hand in hand.

To inspire means literally to breathe in. Both inspiration in the psychological sense and the physical sense are connected. Facing a tough challenge, we naturally take a deep breath to steady our nerves – deep breathing has a calming effect on the mind and body. Top athletes inspire us by pushing the physical boundaries of human physical endeavour with a strategic approach to relaxation. It's not just an add-on when time permits. The temptation is to say 'I can't afford to relax' whereas the truth is that you cannot afford not to. An indispensable part of peak performance psychology and confidence building is the ability to take control of our mental states in order to relax. The tools and techniques in this chapter enable you to do just that. Through a number of personal experiments we consider practical techniques for breathing, relaxation and stress control and the theory behind them, principally the mind–body connection and its implications.

However, before we begin – and given my fondness for the metaphor – let's have another party.

FEELING THE SPACE

Ah, this is the life. All dressed up on an ocean liner with your favourite cocktail in hand, enjoying a nice relaxing evening. However, you are unaware that the ship's orchestra doesn't have time to play all of the requests. Not wanting to disappoint anyone, the conductor decides that they will save time if they play all the notes but miss out the rests – the spaces between the notes. However, two minutes into the programme and you're all praying for an attack of the giant squid!

Often we think of an attractive melody purely in terms of the notes played but, in truth, the beauty resides as much in the stillness, the spaces in between. This is a great metaphor for creating balance in our lives. Action gets results but the insight, the lucidity, derives from stillness. The rests are just as important as hitting the right notes. The breaths are crucial for hitting the high notes.

So without further ado, let's consider the topic of stress.

WHAT IS STRESS?
If asked to define this word, many people would probably start to list all the things that cause them stress. They would also probably name names. People are a major source of stress. Parents, partners, lovers, colleagues, friends, children, pedestrians, motorists, cyclists, shopkeepers, customers, and so on. So that's just about everyone then! It is often our nearest and dearest that have the power to cause us major anxiety. Situations cause us stress too. Our jobs, driving, computers and just about any other form of unpredictable machinery cause us to become tense. Those internal conflicts cause us stress, that is, when we are caught between the proverbial 'rock and a hard place' or 'the devil and the deep blue sea'. Environmental factors such as noise, pollution and temperature cause us strain too. It seems that there is no end to the list of our potential stressors, especially when we're stressed out!

Stress is basically a heightened state of physiological and emotional arousal. Stress affects the way our bodies function, our emotions, our behaviour, our cognitive abilities and the ways we cope. We often think of stress as a bad thing, but broadly speaking there are two types: *distress* and *eustress*.

Distress is the all too familiar bad stuff. We routinely talk about 'being under stress' or 'stressed out'. However there is also good stress. We sometimes use the phrase 'I got a buzz' to refer to an adrenaline rush. We usually perceive this feeling as a good thing, but it is still a form of stress nevertheless and is known as eustress. To illustrate the difference between eustress and distress, think of a catapult. If you place the right amount of stress on the rubber band, close your eye and aim, then you will probably hit your target. However if you put too much stress on the elastic band, it will probably snap back. You miss your target and have to keep your eye closed a lot longer than you expected. Eustress improves performance whereas distress reduces it. So, it makes sense to be able to exert control over the stress in our lives to keep it within limits that are productive rather than destructive.

So, what are your stressors? List your top five here:

1

2

3

4

5

Different things affect different people at different times. It's a matter of the associations (and consequences) we have learned; in addition to an element of personal perception. One person's stressor may be another person's challenge.

So now you have an idea of your stressors let's consider the impact stress can have.

The effects of stress

Overall, we have broadly similar physiological (physical) responses to stress. However, perception plays a strong part. So let's begin by considering the physical and behaviour aspects of stress, with an emphasis on the bad stuff (distress).

Imagine you're relaxing on your yacht taking a leisurely cruise when suddenly, out of the blue, some maniac in a bigger boat looks as though he's heading straight for you. There's no doubt: you're alarmed!

Not surprisingly, this initial response is called the *alarm phase* of stress. It's known as the fight or flight response where we either tackle the stressor head on, or run for cover. As a result the brain fires off impulses to the nervous system that sets off a chain reaction of physical changes:

- We experience an increase in our heart rate, respiration and perspiration rates.
- The pupils in our eyes become wider.
- Sugar is released into the bloodstream for more energy.
- Brain signals then prompt a chain reaction of hormones releasing adrenaline to continue responses started by the nervous system.
- Other hormones are released to maintain these bodily responses.

Phew!

Nevertheless at this stage we still have to process this information in terms of threat or 'rush'. Another important factor is our psychological reaction to the physiological changes. Becoming alarmed by the physical response may lead to further distress. It becomes a vicious cycle.

Back on the ocean, fortunately, you manage to swerve and avoid the other boat and the threat is averted. Yet you still maintain a state of readiness (with higher adrenaline levels) giving you that 'on edge' feeling, just in case there's more than one maniac on the water! This second phase is called the *resistance stage*. In the majority of people, the stressor is usually dealt with during the alarm and resistance stages and then bodily responses return to normal.

It's the long-term (chronic) stress that causes us problems. Basically it leads to a depletion of our body's resources. If our adrenaline levels are maintained at a high point this leads to a reduction in the effectiveness of our immune system, including the depletion of white blood cells. The body under stress is less able to ward off attack from bacteria and viruses. This accounts for why we seem to get colds in times of anxiety when at other times we can be in a room of coughers and splutterers and remain unaffected.

Long-term stress leads to the final phase: *exhaustion*. Falling blood sugar levels are aggravated by disturbed eating patterns (either overeating or undereating). In extreme cases, long-term stress leads to anger and aggression (fight) in some people but results in apathy and depression (flight) in others. Research has shown that health problems associated with chronic stress include asthma, colitis, ulcers, and in extreme cases, heart attacks and cancer. And you say you can't afford to relax!

Confidence boost

There's also another very good reason for you to take control of your relaxation response. Relaxation is the foundation of confidence. Often arrogance is mistaken for confidence. Arrogance comes from insecurity and unassertiveness. Arrogant people work to put others down so they feel better in themselves. Truly confident people put others at ease, because they are relaxed and comfortable with themselves.

The ability to relax, that is to control our physiology, is the basis for peak performance. Lao Tzu got it right when he said: 'To the mind that is still, the whole universe surrenders'.

Stress and performance

The concept of eustress (the good stuff) helps explain why some people seem to thrive on stress when under pressure. Some of us thrive on that little adrenaline rush. It gives us an edge and boosts performance. However, some people make the mistake of thinking that more stress equals ever and ever increasing levels of performance. It doesn't! There's a tipping point at which the effect reverses. A moderate amount of stress sharpens our performance but too much dulls it. This fine line makes it imperative that we are able to exercise control over our responses to stress. There are also some occasions that require a little more stress than others.

Have you ever wondered why it seems to take a long time to get going on tackling some projects? More than likely, these are the less interesting, less demanding tasks that we'd all prefer not to do: the boring stuff. We complain that we need to be 'in the mood' or else wait for the stress of a deadline to kick-start ourselves into action. Different types of tasks need different levels of stress for peak performance: for dull tasks we need slightly higher levels of stress to motivate us. However, the reverse is true for complex tasks. For these we only need a bit of stress. If we get too much it tends to negatively affect our ability to process information. So we can see that it's important to be able to control our stress levels. For the boring tasks we need to psych ourselves up and for the complex tasks we need to be able to calm ourselves down.

So, having briefly considered the connection between stress and performance, let's consider the connection between body and mind.

THE MIND–BODY CONNECTION

Our physical being mirrors our mental state and vice versa. Have you ever noticed when you feel down that your body seems to follow the mood? When we feel down, we tend to lower our heads and look down. In fact the whole seems to mimic our mental slump. We feel dragged down. Conversely, when we feel confident, we look up – head held high – and stand taller. This illustrates the *mind–body connection.*

Our pattern-seeking brains look to establish congruence, a correspondence between body and mind. Our mental moods and bodily states seek to match each other. So, it is possible to exploit this relationship, by deliberately changing our posture. Just try slumping down in your chair right now. You should notice that your mental state starts to move to match the body. Now reverse this by sitting up straight or better still, stand up and stretch. Chin up, chest out, stomach in and stretch you hands to up to the sky and smile. You should notice a slight energy boost. Of course we can extend this to create other states. For instance, if you put your body into a confident posture, it will trick your brain into helping the process along, and you will feel more confident.

The ability to take control of our mental state is not so much under our nose as up it! And I'm not just talking about fresh air! One notable symptom of stress is that our breathing tends to be shallower. When we are relaxed we tend to breathe more deeply and fully. Essentially, by taking control of our breathing patterns we exploit and enjoy the vital connection that exists between our mind and our body.

Every breath you take
All too often we take breathing for granted simply because it seems to take care of itself. And yes, most of the time it does. However, it can involve more than the obligatory in–out, in–out. There are different types of breathing and these can affect your whole body and mind. Let's start with the simplest distinction: shallow breathing and deep breathing.

When we are stressed, afraid or panicked, our breathing tends to become shallower. Physically this means that we do not obtain enough oxygen from each breath and need to breathe faster to compensate. Before we know it we are literally gasping for breath. By contrast, when we are relaxed, happy and contented our breathing becomes fuller and deeper. We experience this with a sigh of contentment, that feeling of just letting go. Deliberate, slow, deeper and fuller breathing puts us in a more relaxed state. So, at this very simplistic level we can control our biological processes. If we relax the body, the mind will be persuaded into following. By controlling our breathing we can influence our response to stressors. Just as stressors induce a stress cycle, we can induce a relaxation cycle consciously by taking control of our breathing and our bodies.

According to James Loehr (a sports psychologist) and Jeffrey Migdow (a medical doctor) in their book *Breathe In Breathe*

Out, the use of breathing techniques may well buy us a few extra breaths! Loehr and Migdow maintain, based on their review of research, that controlled breathing can help to slow down the heart rate, normalize blood pressure, improve digestion, increase energy, improve concentration and memory and may even help make sex more enjoyable. All this from a bit of heavy ... sorry ... I mean *deep* breathing. So, let's consider the basis for the health benefits of controlled breathing.

Take a deep breath
We need oxygen but generally do not use the full capacity of our lungs. Our breathing tends to be shallower using the upper part of the lungs. Due to gravity, the lower part of our lungs has the greatest blood supply. This means that fuller, deeper breathing helps to reduce the number of breaths we take and is more efficient at oxygenating the blood. The heart doesn't have to work as hard and blood pressure doesn't need to be so high. These outcomes are effectively the opposite to those for the stress response. Deep breathing also uses the abdominal muscles and the diaphragm. The diaphragm is a large muscle between the lungs and the abdomen. Together these can help create space to allow the lungs to inflate fully. This process also has a squeezing and massaging effect on the internal organs in the abdomen and this improves blood flow and detoxification (liver function).

In essence, the mind–body connection is driven to congruence and consistency so that bodily states match our mental states and vice versa. So, if your brain receives the signals indicating a relaxed body then the only conclusion can be that you *are* relaxed! Altering you bodily state with deep breathing is a way of short-circuiting the stress response. It's amazing that we can get all of these beneficial effects simply by modifying something we have to do anyway. Few things in life have such a big pay-off.

Now let's pause for a moment to catch our breath.

Three personal experiments

1   Basic abdominal breathing

Here are some instructions for basic deep breathing which will form the basis of the practical exercises (experiments) in this chapter.

Try this:

1   Sit down with your back straight and focus your attention on your breathing.

2   Begin by taking long, slow, deep breaths in through your nose and out through your mouth.

3   As you breath in let the air expand your lungs as fully as possible by letting your abdomen expand.

4   As you breath out, slowly bring in your abdomen (the area around your navel) to squeeze out the air. This should be done slowly and gently. Don't strain. The whole process should be smooth and relaxing.

5   If at any time your mind wanders or thoughts pop into your head, simply acknowledge these thoughts and let them go. Just keep bringing your attention back to your breathing.

6   Do this for ten breaths.

7   So how do you feel? Do you feel more relaxed? Is there any difference? Take a moment to assess this feedback.

8   If you didn't notice much, try doing it again. Scientists often repeat experiments over and over again to test the robustness of the findings. As your own personal development scientist, you may wish to do the same.

Let's take this a step further and introduce the idea of counting to regulate your breathing.

2 Count and hold abdominal breathing
For this exercise, we use the same basic abdominal breathing
technique but add a count to regulate the breathing cycle. We
count to regulate the in and out breath. We also add a pause
by holding our breath in between.

Special note: At this point, you need to decide whether holding the breath is suitable for you. So, if you have any medical
conditions such as respiratory, blood pressure, heart problems, or any other medical condition, then consult your
doctor. None of this is a substitute for medical advice. In
the meantime, omit the breath-holding instructions in this
book and just pause for a moment.

The instructions for 'count and hold abdominal breathing'
are:

1   The breathing is regulated by a counted ratio of 8:4:8. If
    you can't manage this, try 6:3:6 or 4:2:4.
2   Breathe in as before but this time to the mental count of
    eight.
3   Hold for the mental count of four.
4   Breathe out as before to the mental count of eight.
5   Do this for ten breaths.
6   If at anytime thoughts pop into your head, don't fight them
    or resent them, just acknowledge them and let them drift
    away. Keep bringing your mind back to your breathing,
    gently.

Take time to do this breathing exercise throughout the day Ideally, aim for three times per day.

So how did that feel? How do you feel? It's amazing that something so simple that we have to do anyway can be adapted, with very little time or effort, to such beneficial effects.

So far we have talked about the brain in terms of its capacity to interpret and create links. Let's consider the physical changes to the brain brought about by relaxation.

Brain waves

In a moment, close your eyes and take a few long slow deep breaths then open your eyes. Do it now.

Ah! You're back. You've just achieved something quite amazing. Simply by closing your eyes you have altered your brain waves. Taking a deep breath did the same and compounded the effect. When we are awake and alert our brain produces *beta waves* and when we are relaxed it produces *alpha waves*. Both closing your eyes and breathing deeply trigger more alpha waves. So, the old idea of taking a deep breath before a challenge actually does help to steady our nerves, or rather, it steadies the waves.

Let's get back to the buoyant ambience of the cocktail party and I'll explain the process there.

All together now

Back at the cocktail party the orchestra is sticking to the programme of playing all of the notes and rests. The whole room buzzes with many small groups of people engaged in different animated conversations and discussions. Suddenly the orchestra breaks into 'Relax' by Frankie Goes to Hollywood, that timeless classic!

Now, imagine that each person at the cocktail party represents a brain cell. Before the orchestra began playing, there was no synchronization amongst the crowd of people engaging in numerous different conversations in small groups. This hive of activity is much the same as our waking states in everyday life where stimuli bombard us from all directions. In this state of high activation our brains produce *beta waves*. However, when the orchestra begins, the crowd all begin to sing in unison. With the crowd synchronized the message is much simpler. In this state of 'togetherness' and lower activation, our brains produce *alpha waves*. Essentially when we get ready to go to sleep, our brains begin to switch off from the day's hustle and bustle and sing the 'alpha wave lullaby'.

It's quite remarkable that this relatively modern scientific knowledge was understood by ancient religions that taught meditation practices. Chanting during meditation is an external representation of what happens in the brain as we relax.

In Chapter Two we discussed the learning cycle so let's consider briefly what's going on inside our brains and how this relates to learning to relax and control our stress response.

Making connections
Brain cells, known as neurons, are tiny information transmitters and processors. We have different neurons for different jobs:

- *Sensory neurons* specialize in gathering information from our senses of sight, sound, taste, smell and touch.
- *Motor neurons* control muscle movement.
- In between lie all the other 100 billion neurons that take care of the perception, learning, remembering, decision making and controlling of complex behaviours.

Put simply, neurons communicate with each other with squirts of chemicals. There's a lot of squirting. It's busy in there! As we learn, these little squirts form pathways (neural pathways). The more we repeat the learning building associations (classical conditioning) and learning consequences (operant conditioning) more squirts mean more clearly defined pathways. Round and round the learning cycle with action (squirt), reflection (squirt), theorizing (squirt) and planning (squirt). Think of a drip that becomes a trickle that becomes a stream that becomes a river. Practice, with good feedback, does indeed make perfect.

By taking control of your breathing and your relaxation response you are effectively changing your nervous system. You change your filters and in effect 'rewire' your brain. Relaxation triggers more alpha wave activity in the brain. Mind over clutter! So, by adopting a meditation practice (breathing and relaxation) we essentially mirror outwardly what we want to happen inwardly. The brain likes patterns. We cannot be anxious and relaxed at the same time. The brain likes to establish congruence between the mind and body. So, if we relax the body, the mind will follow.

Stress is often accompanied by a sense of being out of control. The opposite of stress, in the form of strategic relaxation, is taking control. The secret is to practise regularly to reinforce the new conditioning in the brain. Let's do just that with my two minute stress buster.

Personal experiment: two minute stress buster
This mini stress buster is very simple but deceptively powerful. Do this three times throughout the day. Every hour on the hour would be ideal, or if not whenever you can manage it.

Try this:

1   Stand upright with your feet shoulder width apart, head up and eyes closed and do seven counted abdominal breaths.
2   Breathe in fully through your nose and smile.
3   Hold for the mental count of four.
4   Breathe out through your mouth and say 'aaaaaah' in the form of a sigh.
5   Do this seven to ten times.

If you are not able to get privacy to do the 'aaaaaah', then substitute your one word prayer of 'relax' or 'calm', and just say it mentally. Whatever version you opt for, you can maximize the effects by suspending your disbelief and 'acting in to it'. Exaggerate it. Try doing this every day for a week. A month would be even better. At the very least do it during the time you're reading this book.

At the end of the period reflect on what you have noticed. Did it work for you? What can you do with your feedback? If it's working for you, how can you incorporate it into your daily life? If it's not working, how can you amend it to make it work for you?

Let's take this a step further and consider the topic of meditation.

MEDITATION

Present-moment awareness

No doubt the word 'meditation' conjures up images and associations for you. These may be positive or negative, based on what you've learned and your perceptions. If you see meditation as a load of New Age mumbo-jumbo, then your perceptual filters will tune in to the information that supports that view. However, in psychological terms, it represents control and choice. It doesn't have to have any of the trappings normally associated with mysticism.

Modern life is so frantic that we rarely have the chance to switch off. Meditation can provide us with the means to fulfil this choice and control the 'noise'. Think of it like a remote control for your television. You can choose to turn down the volume, switch channels or switch off. That's your choice.

In the introduction I commented that I didn't experience enough sunrises. So, when did you last see the sun rise? When did you take time out to watch the sun set? When I'm on holiday and everyone comes out to watch the sun set, as though we are all joined in a collective meditation. There's no religious dogma, no airy-fairy nonsense. Everyone is in a pure state of present-moment awareness, just kind of being there.

So here are four more personal experiments for you to test out:

1 Sunrises and sunsets (meditation)
Sometime this week, make an appointment with yourself in your diary to watch a sunrise and a sunset. It doesn't have to be on the same day. When watching them, don't analyse anything; just experience it. Be there in the present moment. If thoughts or worries intrude, just acknowledge them and let them go. Just be there, be still and take it in. This is meditation.

Take some long slow deep breaths. Stay there for as long as you wish. If you want to reflect on your thoughts and feelings afterwards, that's up to you. Does this fit in with your idea of what meditation is supposed to be like? Now try other experiences such as a walk in the park, or by the river, or try sitting outside a café just for the sake of being there. Make a note in your diary to meditate in this way at least once a week.

One of the issues commonly encountered is intruding thoughts. People have high expectations and assume if their minds don't become totally still, it's not working or they're not 'doing it right'. This is not the case. Meditation is an ongoing practice. If thoughts do pop into your head, the next experiment provides a way of dealing with them, that is, simply to acknowledge the thoughts and observe them.

2 'Just being there' meditation

If your mind is a pool, then your thoughts are the ripples and waves. They rise and fall with spaces of stillness in between. As thoughts flow into your mind, simply observe them. Don't focus on the content, just acknowledge the beginning of the thought and also notice when it ends. Observe the stillness that follows. Repeat this for any subsequent thoughts. You will notice that the thoughts become less frequent and the periods of stillness increase. Now close your eyes, take long slow deep breaths and simply observe. Just be there as a witness.

Now let's consider a meditation practice that takes into account some of the basic psychological principles we have discussed so far, in particular classical conditioning (learning by association).

3 Simple no-frills meditation practice (one-word prayer)

For this exercise you will need to think of a word or phrase that will act as affirmation of your intention to relax. You can think of it as a one-word prayer or a one-word trigger. So you might choose simply to use 'relax' or 'calm', 'peace' or 'still'. The word 'calmer' is good as it suggests progressive, deeper relaxation. The choice is yours. Once you have your word, familiarize yourself with the instructions and try this exercise.

1   Sit comfortably in a place where you are not likely to be disturbed.
2   Close your eyes and take a long slow deep breath, in through your nose.
3   Hold your breath to the mental count of four.
4   As you breathe out through your mouth mentally repeat your chosen word (you can say it out loud if you want to).
5   If thoughts pop into your head just acknowledge them, let them go and bring yourself back to your breathing and your trigger word.
6   Do this for at least ten breaths.

I recommend that you try the above meditation a few times before progressing to the next one. When we experience stress it tends to manifest itself as tension in various parts of our bodies. This exercise adds progressive muscle relaxation for the whole body.

4   One-word prayer alternate version (with added muscle monitoring)
The added ingredient to this exercise is progressive relaxation of your body from the tips of your toes to the top of your head. Read the instructions through a few times then try the exercise.

1   Take three abdominal breaths, with your one-word prayer on the out breath.

2   Begin to focus on each part of your body, starting with the toes of your left foot.

3   As you breath in, tense your toes.

4   Pause for the mental count of four.

5   As you breathe out, release the tension and mentally say 'relax'.

6   Repeat this for all parts of your body, working upwards.

7   Move up to your calf, then thigh, then move onto the right leg.

8   In turn, tense your buttocks, your abdomen, your chest, fingers and hands, arms (each arm in turn), shoulders, neck, face and scalp.

9   When you have worked on all of your body, do three more abdominal breaths, repeating the word 'relax' or your one-word prayer.

These exercises condition us to make associations (see Chapter Two). With the one-word prayer exercise (with or without muscle monitoring) the chosen word becomes associated with the relaxed state. Practised regularly and frequently this word or phrase will acquire the power to interrupt your stress response just by closing your eyes briefly and saying it. In the initial stages, do this meditation two to three times per day (morning, after lunch and evening) for just a few minutes. Do it every day for a week. Assess the results.

Pick 'n' mix

Now that we've reviewed the basic techniques you can experiment with the relaxation exercises, creating different combinations that work for you. You may wish to create different combinations for different times. You also may consider using relaxation music during your meditation exercises. Many people find that these help focus the attention and enhance the experience. There are numerous CDs on the market including compilations of Western Classical pieces (usually *adagio* movements) for meditation.

Meditation, in essence, is a combination of breathing, relaxation and focused attention. Physically experiencing a sunrise, a sunset or walks in the park are all forms of meditation. However, when these aren't a practical option there's always our imagination to fall back on. Putting ourselves in a relaxed state and mentally recreating a favourite scene can be enormously relaxing. Take yourself on an imaginary cruise to your favourite places. This is meditation too. In Chapter Seven we will be considering the strategic use of imagination for supporting our goal setting and skills development. In the meantime, lets consider some more tangible ways to combat stress.

A bit of fun

The popular computer game The Sims offers an excellent model for life balance and peak performance. It's a simulation game where the player creates and controls a neighbourhood, helps individual characters build homes, get jobs, make friends and find romance. The characters (Sims) have personalities with motives and needs that must be met if they are to be happy. As well as personal development and career progression, they have basic needs such as hunger, comfort, hygiene, bladder, energy, social and environmental needs and fun. There's nothing like a bit of fun to put us in a relaxed state.

The medicinal effects of laughter are well documented. In fact, a really good laugh has much of the same therapeutic effects on the body, as does deep abdominal breathing. Ideally we should try to find something to laugh about every day, even if it's just watching a comedy DVD instead of a horror. A daily laugh helps reduce stress, improve respiration (so you gain even more out of your deep breathing), it lowers the stress chemicals and releases the 'pleasure chemical' dopamine. It's often said that laughter is the best medicine. So don't live your life in the placebo group!

What do *you* do to have fun? Is fun a luxury or a necessity? Begin by making a list of everyday things that are fun for you. Do you enjoy reading, listening to music, painting, going to the gym or taking dance classes? Do you have any hobbies? What about going to the cinema, the theatre, a concert, learning to play a musical instrument or playing a computer game? It can be any activity that you can totally lose yourself in. Furthermore, do you book fun time in your diary? Ponder on these questions for the moment. In the next chapter we will consider the subjects of life balance and of goal setting.

If physical exercise is your idea of fun then you can also reap the benefits of its stress-busting effects. At the physiological level, regular exercise provides an outlet for the fight or flight responses, helping us to burn up stress chemicals. It's also good for getting away from stress-provoking circumstances for a while and helps distract us from reviewing negative thinking.

In short, exercise can help us to retune our perceptual filters. Of course, as we know, it has numerous health benefits such as helping to reduce blood pressure, reduce cholesterol, improve cardiovascular fitness, maintain a healthy weight and improve muscle tone. It also helps release those good chemicals in the brain such as *serotonin*. This is an important chemical that contributes to a range of functions, including sleep and wake cycles, libido, appetite and mood. Furthermore, exercise has been found to be effective in helping to combat anxiety and depression. I'm adding these to my list of reasons to go back to the gym.

The Sims computer game is about taking control of imaginary lives. If the characters' needs are not met they become tired or cranky and, in the most extreme cases, they can die. It's a *sim*plistic model (excuse the pun) but it does highlight two main points relevant to our seemingly more complicated human existence: balance and control. Indeed much of what we have discussed so far highlights control as the antidote to stress.

TAKING THE CONTROLS: A QUESTION OF BALANCE

Stress is more than just a collection of physiological responses and some writers emphasize the importance of the dynamic effect of environment on the individual. An overriding factor is our individual perception of the demands facing us. From this view, stress results when we feel out of control and the perceived demands outweigh perceived capability to deal with them. This explains why some people rise to the challenge whilst others sink at the first sign of pressure.

Stress and control: externalizers vs internalizers

Our ability to cope with stress often depends on whether we see ourselves as controlling our lives or whether our lives control us. Not surprisingly, when we feel as if we are out of control, we are likely to feel stressed. As in many areas of our lives we tend to make sense of the world using general all-purpose scripts. If we habitually use one particular script it becomes part of our personality make-up. In psychology this characteristic is known as *locus of control* and two types have been identified: *internalizers* and *externalizers*. They represent opposing views of the world.

Internalizers perceive themselves to have a greater degree of personal control. They see control as coming from the inside. They are the active agents and are more likely to agree with these statements:

- *I am the captain of my ship.*
- *I am responsible for charting my own course in life.*
- *If you want something done properly, you have to do it yourself.*

By contrast, externalizers are more likely to view themselves as being controlled by external factors. They see control of their lives coming from the outside. They are the passive recipients and are more likely to agree with these statements:

- *We are all victims of fate, tossed about on a sea of indifference.*
- *God or the government is there to solve our problems.*
- *If it's meant to happen it will happen.*

Take a moment to think how your perspective might differ if you habitually viewed the world as an externalizer versus an internalizer. Consider the two sets of statements. Which set applies to you? Research into perceived control and stress indicates, on average, that internalizers cope better with stress than do externalizers. Internalizers see themselves in control rather than being controlled. As such internalizers are more likely to take action, whereas externalizers are more likely to rely on fate. The guiding principles of *insight, ownership* and *action* emphasise an internal locus (origin) of control. Internalizers take ownership and take action. By contrast, the *cosmic ordering* approach has a stronger emphasis on external control. Research into stress and coping favours an *insight, ownership* and *action* type approach.

However, this is not an all-out prescription to become a control freak. In the next section, we consider the virtue of balance.

Type A/Type B

Meyer Friedman and Ray Rosehan looked at the links between patterns of behaviour and health, in particular the incidence of heart disease. Their findings pointed to two broad types of behavioural patterns: Type A and Type B.

People with Type A behaviour appear to be more driven. They are ambitious, competitive, alert, impatient and somewhat aggressive. Their speech is hurried, they gesture frequently and often interrupt if people take too long to get to the point. They tend always to be in a hurry and are competitive in leisure events. Physiologically they show long term (chronic) high levels of arousal, so tend to live life in the resistance stage of stress, always on the edge. Even though their behaviours have detrimental health effects, Type A people are often highly successful and so their activities are not discouraged.

In contrast Type B people do not appear so driven. Although they may be equally ambitious, they do not allow it to dominate their lives. Instead they balance time for ambition with time for family and friends and choose leisure pursuits that are less competitive. Overall people exhibiting Type A behaviour are more than two and a half times more likely to develop heart disease than those showing Type B behaviour.

Take a moment to consider the two descriptions. Which type are you? Do you take time to smell the roses or are you too busy fighting a War of the Roses? Research into why some people cope with a catalogue of stressful events and others break down under the slightest pressure has revealed three main factors: *control*, *commitment* and *challenge*. This resonates with the principles of *ownership* and *action* in this book. People who cope better under adverse stress tend to be Type B internalizers. They are more likely to feel in control of their lives, are more action-focused and lead balanced lives. They also tend to be more oriented to challenges and change. This fits in very well with the next chapter on goal setting (commitment and challenge). In this we will consider creating life-balance and also how to set goals that stretch us.

To reap the benefits of these insights, we don't necessarily have to make grand changes overnight. We can make a big difference by tacking the small stuff. It all adds up. In the next approach to stress we do that just that.

Hassles and uplifts

No doubt we've all experienced a stressful life event or significant change in our lives that threw us off course. Things such as a change of job, ill heath, the break up of a relationship or the loss of a loved one can overwhelm us. Then there are times when the smallest things get under our skin. The vending machine that swallows our money, the rude shopkeeper, someone who doesn't bother to say thanks when we open the door, and so on. These are the petty niggles in life that drive us to distraction. They seem to stack up until we experience the final straw that breaks the camel's back. Take a moment to think of your petty niggles. What are the little hassles in life that wear you down and spoil your day?

Daily hassles

Now think of all the little uplifts in life that make your day. It might be a cheery word from the local shopkeeper; maybe someone opens a door for you, smiles at you or gives you a compliment.

Daily uplifts

At the end of the day, whether you consider it a good day or one of 'those' days may be based on a few seemingly trivial events. In psychology this is known as the *hassles and uplifts theory* of stress. According to the theory, at the end of each day we create a mental balance sheet of our overall 'feel' for the day. If the hassles outweigh the uplifts then we've had a bad day. If it's the other way round we've had a good day. Too many lousy days lead us to feel as if we are worn down and worn out. However, when we start to analyse the hassles and uplifts theory, it suggests that we have a greater control over good days and bad days than we maybe realize. Often it only takes a couple of things to frame the day in a negative light and, likewise, just a few to turn it around again. This works in much the same way as perceptual filters. So imagine that the shopkeeper is rude to you first thing in the morning. This sets up a negative mindset and everything just seems to go downhill from there. The idea that it's going to be one of those days makes us more likely to pay attention to the stuff that confirms this hypothesis. In effect we become primed for the bad stuff which stacks up throughout the day. So now consider the reverse. The shopkeeper pays us a compliment or tells a little joke and we end up having a great day. Of course it's inevitable that some days are going to be worse than others. The good news is that we can limit the effects by deliberately framing our day with positive uplifts. This is exactly the principle behind the gratitude and anticipation exercise in Chapter One. Perhaps surprisingly, some research indicates that the build-up of daily hassles is a better predictor of stress-related ill health than critical life events. Again, taking care of the small stuff can have a dramatic effect on the way we view the world.

We can become daily uplift internalizers by creating small, positive daily events that stack up to affect our overall feel for the day. A bit of fun here, a bit of relaxation there, a breathing exercise or two, a moment of meditation and the view of a sunset are all ways of increasing our quota of daily uplifts.

In the introduction to this book, I said that the expectation to rise and shine everyday is perhaps too much of a tall order; well, maybe it's not anymore. Here is a daily uplift in the form of a simple breathing technique to get you started in the morning. It's appropriately called *The Rise and Shine Breath*.

ONE MORE PERSONAL EXPERIMENT: RISE AND SHINE
You'll be happy to learn that *The Rise and Shine Breath* is performed whilst still enjoying the comfort of your bed. Read it through a few times to familiarize yourself with the technique. Here's my version, which combines deep breathing with an early morning stretch:

1 Breathe in through your nose with your arms clenched in – fists at your shoulders as if you are about to lift weights (chest press). Smile as you breathe in.
2 Push out your stomach as you breath in.
3 Now breathe out through your mouth, making an 'aaaah' sound like a sigh, and push your arms up to the ceiling. Open your hands and stretch out your fingers.
4 Pull your arms back to your shoulders with clenched fists. Pull down as if there is resistance and breathe in as before.
5 Do about seven to ten of these.
6 Smile. Now breathe in deeply (through your nose) and hold your breath for the count of ten seconds or a little longer if you can comfortably do so.
7 Breath out forcefully through your mouth whilst pulling your stomach in.
8 Do three of these.
9 It's now time to sit up.
10 Repeat points 1 to 4 sitting up. Do another seven to ten of these.
11 Optional extra: do another seven to ten breaths standing up.
12 You are now ready to face the world! OK, so it may not be enough to conquer the world but it should summon up the will to put the kettle on!

Right! Let's draw together all of the themes for this chapter and ask 'what is your relaxation protocol?'

Your relaxation protocol
With the insights gained from this chapter, the challenges are to take ownership of your basic physiological states and create an action plan. Some may argue (probably Type As) that in order to attain our peak in this rat race we can't afford to stop or relax, let alone sit navel gazing in mystical meditative states. Professional athletes are perceived as people who push themselves to the limit rather than taking it easy. However, top athletes make relaxation one of their core skills. In Chapter Two we talked about recharging our batteries. Relaxation helps us do just that at both psychological and physiological levels – leading to less stress, more happiness and better performance. Relaxation and meditation help focus the attention and help prevent us from mentally rehearsing worries and anxieties. It's about taking control of our lives at the most fundamental level. Taking time to re-energize is not a luxury, just as eating, drinking and going to the lavatory are not added extras. The tools and techniques in this chapter are simple and effective practical ways in which we can create balance in our lives.

The use of strategic relaxation represents a commitment to take responsibility to give yourself those daily uplifts. The amount of time you invest in relaxation will have a knock-on effect and energize all aspects of your life. So, what's your plan? Try the experiments in this chapter, using the zero to ten scale to measure the before and after levels of relaxation.

In the next chapter we consider the concept of creating a balanced life through simple goal-setting techniques. In the meantime, what are seven things that would make this a better day, a better week? Which of the simple techniques will you commit to each day? Let's start with a list of those daily uplifts:

1

2

3

4

5

6

7

Now take action. Do them!

DRYING OFF

Review: In this chapter we pondered the physiological aspects of stress and introduced relaxation as the basis for peak performance. Relaxation and meditation techniques are key in interrupting the stress cycle. The interventions can have beneficial effects on our physical and psychological states and abilities. Daily uplifts and daily hassles have been highlighted as a way in which we can take control over each day. This sense of control, and a commitment to balance, are key factors for coping with daily stresses and a basis for building confidence. Plain sailing is easier on a calmer sea.

In the next chapter we will consider new challenges in the form of goal setting.

REFLECTION (*REFL-ACTION*)

1 **INSIGHT**: What are the three most important things you learned in this chapter?

(i)

(ii)

(iii)

2 **OWNERSHIP**: What impact has this had in terms of the way you think about your accountability for your life and goals?

3 **ACTION**: What action does this inspire you to take to make a positive change in your life? What personal experiment might you conduct to get feedback and insight?

Chapter Six

GETTING IN THE FLOW OF THINGS

Ready, steady, goal!

If one does not know to which port one is sailing, no wind is favourable.

Seneca

I find the great thing in this world is not so much where we stand, as in what direction we are moving – we must sail sometimes with the wind and sometimes against it – but we must sail, and not drift, nor lie at anchor.

Oliver Wendell Holmes Junior

As we voyage along through life,
Tis the act of the soul that determines the goal,
And not the calm or the strife.

Ella Wheeler Wilcox

DIPPING A TOE

Preview: In this chapter we'll ponder the benefits of goal setting and consider various tools and techniques for creating watertight action plans for goal setting. We also look at motivation, linking goals to values and connection between goals and happiness.

A TEST OF RESOLVE

Resolutions for resolution

Each year, seized by the promise of 'New Year: New You', many of us make our New Year's resolutions. All too often, the motivation wanes and the action soon fizzles out. However, it doesn't have to be this way.

Looking at the different meanings for resolution they incorporate the principles of *insight, ownership* and *action* as well as *persistence.* A resolution is a decree or declaration. It is a promise, an oath, a pledge and a vow. Resolution means determination, steadfastness, tenacity and firmness. A resolution is the upshot, the solution, the answer. It's the positive outcome or the preferred end-state.

The aim of this chapter is to consider resolutions in the form of goals, which live up to all of these shades of meaning. We apply the insights gained so far through a series of tried and tested tools and techniques to transform vague promises into well-formed action plans for positive, lasting change.

The attitudes of ownership and 'taking it personally' help us become fit and ready for action. So, are you ready? Let's see.

FIT AND READY FOR GOAL SETTING?

Let's begin with a test that plays devil's advocate with ten negative statements to assess your readiness for goal setting. For each of these statements just answer (circle) true or false. For the purposes of this test, there is no maybe.

Test of ownership: are you ready for action?

1   True or False? I've done all right so far, so why bother with goal setting now?

2   True or False? If I achieve my goals, people will expect even more of me.

3   True or False? I get weighed down by the idea of a constant, lifelong pursuit of goals, and yet more goals.

4   True or False? If I don't try then I won't fail.

5   True or False? I don't need to set goals.

6   True or False? Things tend to work out as fate intended, whether or not I set goals.

7   True or False? I don't want to feel constrained by goal chasing.

8   True or False? Goals are just another way of getting us to tow society's line.

9   True or False? All the energy I spend setting goals may as well be used to get the job done.

10 True or False? I'm just not a goal setting kind of person.

Scoring

- Mostly False: This suggests that you are ready to take the plunge and set goals. Otherwise, you may have already been routinely setting and achieving goals. Hopefully this chapter will help to strengthen your resolve.

- Mostly True: On face value this would indicate that you are not ready to set goals. However, the mere fact that you bothered to take the test suggests that there's a faint glimmer of interest. Perhaps you are more inclined to let the hand of fate sort it out. That isn't resolution; that's resignation.

So, if you have still not received a cosmic reply to your message in a bottle (The Intro), I have a proposition for you. While you're waiting, why not get some practice in creating action plans (as a personal experiment) and test them out. This doubles your chances of success. If you achieve your goals under your own steam *and* the cosmic order comes through too, you can sell the surplus results on e-Bay! You can't lose! It's a win-win-win situation.

Throughout this book is the theme of taking it personally. As a teenager I had a conversation with my grandfather that has stayed with me throughout my life.

IN THE FLOW

As I chatted with my granddad one Saturday afternoon, I asked him if he had any regrets. He had two: getting a tattoo and not planning for his retirement.

The second one puzzled me for many years. After all, we often think about retirement as a time when we finally get to relax, put our feet up and do absolutely nothing. Of course, this may be some people's idea of bliss. It wasn't for my grandfather.

It wasn't until I discovered the work of psychologist Mihaly Csikszentmihalyi (pronounced 'chick-SENT-me-high') that my grandfather's comments made sense. Csikszentmihalyi's classic work *Flow* explains how happiness is not something we leave to chance. We need to set happiness goals. Being 'in flow' is that state of being completely and utterly absorbed in something. We lose ourselves in the moment and lose all sense of time. My grandfather used to read a great deal, in fact he would read just about anything he could lay his hands on, even my comics. I always thought that was great. I guess he was the role model for my love of learning. He's also the main reason I never got a tattoo (well, apart from the pain).

Many of my friends ask me when I'm going to stop taking courses and learning. My answer is usually short and to the point: 'When I'm dead'. Blunt but true! Like it or not, we learn from our first breath in, to our final breath out. I prefer to take ownership and exert control over the lessons I learn. I can't imagine retiring from learning. I'll always be setting myself new challenges, going on courses, teaching, reading, and writing for as long as I'm above ground. Why? The answer is simple: this approach to life helps me live to my values and play to my strengths. In short, it makes me happy. The research shows that it's not just me who feels this way.

Many of us experience flow when we play computer games. We lose all sense of time and hours seem to pass like minutes. For Csikszentmihalyi, the more time we spend in flow, the happier we are. The key element with computer games is the pursuit of skill and mastery. Think about any skill that you voluntarily try to master and the hours you put in to achieve it. Suddenly you 'get it'. Everything falls into place. How do you feel at that moment? You hit a peak because you have pursued a peak experience. It's something we are motivated to do as children, whether it's walking a few extra steps or surpassing our personal best. As Robert Browning says 'Our reach should exceed our grasp'. Being in flow is about investing ourselves in realistic but demanding goals in line with our values and strengths. Setting 'reaching' goals helps us to reach ourselves and, in the process, grasp happiness.

So, before we consider goal setting, let's consider what can go wrong with New Year's resolutions and how we can go the distance with our goals.

GOING THE DISTANCE

Every New Year our attention is drawn to personal change, which we translate into intention in the form of resolutions. So, why do they fizzle out? What's the problem?

Well, we start with good intentions and take action, but the problem is that, more often than not, we simply don't have a well thought-out action plan. We need a well-defined target, not something fuzzy, vague, and 'over there somewhere'. So, let's begin by looking at six common problems with New Year's resolutions, and then put them right.

Negativity

Some of the classic New Year's resolutions are about 'cutting out', 'cutting down', 'losing' or 'giving up'; for instance, giving up sugar or losing weight. However, ideally goals should be positively phrased, focusing on what we want to move towards. Both of the aforementioned goals have a negative connotation. Aiming for your ideal weight is a better idea as it focuses on attainment and not loss. Instead of giving up favourite foods think of increasing the variety of foods. This way you can still eat your favourites but it is more likely to be in the context of a balanced diet. Wherever possible we should aim for positively stated goals.

Vagueness

New Year's resolutions point in the general direction of the goal, but the goal is not pinpointed. It's difficult to hit a target if it's not clearly defined. Perennial favourites include: vowing to get healthy, getting toned and honed, going to the gym, giving up smoking and losing weight. There's nothing wrong with anyone of them, in fact my favourites are amongst them.

The problem is that such goals are one big amorphous lump of intention. What exactly does 'get healthy' mean? It's rather like the heat-seeking missile getting instructions 'over there somewhere'. To hit a target it helps if we know where it is and what it looks like.

Consider exactly what you want to accomplish. Targets may become clearer if bigger goals are broken down into smaller goals. Goals are easier to achieve if they focus on specific behaviours. Smaller 'get healthy' goals might be broken down into eating five portions of fresh fruit and vegetables each day and drinking seven glasses (200ml) of water each day, and so on. Target specific actions.

Immeasurable

New Year's resolutions do not contain a measure of success. So, how will you know when you've reached the goal? Ask yourself some 'how' questions. How much? How many? How often? How will I know when I've achieved it? Can you put a number on it? Goals need to be measurable.

Breaking goals into sub-goals or milestones also helps build motivation as you tick off those milestones. A goal of 'going to the gym *more often*' isn't easily measurable. But 'going to the gym twice per week for an hour each time' most definitely is. It provides a clear idea of the commitment. We also know when we're on track and when we're not.

Unachievable

Often we psych ourselves up for New Year's resolutions. It becomes a case of 'now or never', which tends to lead us to set overreaching goals. Goals need to stretch us but still be within our potential. If it's too easy we become bored but if it's too difficult we give up and it dents our confidence. Achievability is about knowing one's own strengths and limitations (insight).

Unrealistic

New Year's resolutions may be well within our capability but unrealistic when we take into account existing resources and competing demands. For instance, it is unrealistic to vow to go to the gym everyday for five hours per day if you've never set foot in one before. Also, it would not be realistic to go on a diet on Christmas Eve, or before any cultural feast or with a run of parties on the horizon. Another common mistake is trying to tackle too many things at once such as deciding to give up smoking, drinking and chocolate, going to the gym and going on a diet, all on the same day! That's going to be a very long day. It is more realistic to focus on one of these at a time. Another common problem is trying to plan every minute (or every calorie) of every day forever! It is not sustainable in the long term. Being realistic also means being flexible.

Open-ended

The final stumbling block with New Year's resolutions is that they rarely have a time scale or a target date. Often, they are just open-ended intentions that seem to stretch out into infinity. If we don't set a time frame then there is no sense of urgency to the goal. End-states need end dates.

There are two ways that we can set realistic target dates:

- *Count back*: Begin with a fixed date in mind. When you know what you want to achieve and have realistic milestones then you simply count back from the target date to the present.

This process will act as a confirmation as to whether the target date is achievable and realistic. If not, you need to use the feedback and adjust the date or modify the goal.

- *Make a prediction*: If you don't have a fixed date in mind, then count forwards adding up your realistic milestones to set the final date. Remember that the milestones need to stretch you (a little) too.

Together, these points provide a tighter structure for our goals, offering a clear and unambiguous basis for creating a workable action plan. So, let's look at how we can use this feedback to create a memorable formula for well-formed outcomes – predictable preferred end-states!

Well-formed outcomes
Introducing SMARTER goals
Goals need to be well formed. To achieve this we can use the simple acronym SMARTER. I've included alternatives for each term to give a more comprehensive definition of the SMARTER formula:

- **S** for Specific (also significant and stretching)
- **M** for Measurable (also milestones, meaningful and motivational)
- **A** for Achievable (also action-orientated)
- **R** for Realistic (also relevant, reasonable, rewarding and results-oriented)
- **T** for Time-bound (also tangible and trackable)
- **E** for Enthusiastic and positively worded
- **R** for Regularly Reviewed

Before you begin to put SMARTER into practice, let's discuss start dates for goals. We seem to invest a great deal in the first day of the New Year.

The best time to start?
The first day of a new year is brimming with symbolism and significance as we ring out the old and ring in the new. The whole 'brand new year, brand new you' philosophy certainly gets us started, but it's often not enough to carry us through. And, if it is the only thing that's driving us, it could become more of a millstone than a motivation. So, if we stumble, or hit an obstacle, the temptation is to give up and try again next year. However, it's important to realize that one day is much like any other as far as goal setting is concerned. Don't let an arbitrary date be a setback. If you stumble along the way, just apply the principles of *insight, ownership* and *action*. Take stock, review the feedback, make your adjustments, take a deep breath and get right back in there! If you need a rule or a reason to pick a new day, try my *rule of the next available day that contains a vowel*, and move on! It's a good enough reason as any.

Later in this chapter we will discuss the question of motivation in greater depth, but in the meantime let's consider setting some goals.

GOALS: THE LONG, THE SHORT AND THE TALL
Goals can be anything from magnificent, life-changing, character-building, soul-defining aspirations to those all-too-often overlooked simple daily uplifts (Chapter Five), and anything else in between. Whether it's climbing Everest, swimming with dolphins, sailing round the world, weeding the garden or buy-

ing a new pair of shoes, we can set goals in just about any area of our lives.

To put ourselves 'in flow' we need to set goals that stretch us. They need to be challenging enough to take us out of our comfort zones. However, sometimes when we have a busy schedule just fitting in a daily uplift can be a challenge. So, before we focus on the substantial goals, first let's look at the small stuff.

A question of balance

If asked, 'Do you lead a balanced life?' I guess most people would say 'It depends what you mean by balanced'. To lead a balanced life implies that we have to work at it; if we don't take the lead then life ends up leading us! Staff development departments run courses on work–life balance. However, no one seems to notice or care that there are only two factors in this equation. On one side we have work and on the other side the rest of what makes up our lives. It's hardly a good balance. What we need to do is broaden the scope in all areas of our lives.

The following *life balance analysis* exercise has two main components. It offers a number of life areas to consider and requires an assessment of our satisfaction with each. Sometimes, some areas of our lives get more attention than others by necessity. As the saying goes 'the squeaky wheel gets greased'. For the purposes of this exercise, and goal setting, I offer ten life areas for consideration. However, if any of these don't work for you, then replace them with your own. My suggestions are:

1 Health and well-being – any aspect of physical and psychological health.
2 Wealth and finances.
3 Home and environment.
4 Fun (use of leisure time, hobbies, interests, laughter and so on).
5 Relaxation.
6 Support network (friends and family).
7 Intimacy.
8 Vocation (job, career, calling, professional life).
9 Personal development (opportunities for learning and growth).
10 Spirituality (however you define it) – you may want to replace this with 'living your top values'.

In the life coaching partnership, the client sets the agenda and the coach provides the tools and strategy for change. So long as these goals aren't illegal and don't cause harm to others, as Shakespeare said 'the world's your oyster'. In keeping with the theme of personal experiments, I have devised an exercise involving a row of test tubes, one for each life area. To complete the exercise:

1 Think about what factors contribute to your satisfaction in this area of your life (test tube).
2 What detracts from your satisfaction?
3 Now give this area of your life a satisfaction rating from zero to ten. To indicate your satisfaction make a mark for the water level across the test tube, using these guidelines:

- If you are 'totally unsatisfied' you will not make a mark at all.
- If you are only 'slightly satisfied' you will make a mark around one or two on the test tube.
- If 'moderately satisfied' you would make a mark at around three to five.
- Marks of six or seven represent 'high satisfaction'.
- Eight and nine represent 'very high satisfaction'.
- A rating of ten means that your test tube 'positively runneth over'!

There are no right and wrong answers and no 'oughts', 'shoulds' or 'musts'. The aim is not to compare yourself with others or to any external standard. All that matters is your own personal satisfaction. In this exercise it is OK to use fractions. Now go right to the chart and complete it before continuing.

The completed chart offers a visual summary of your satisfaction across the main areas of your life. Beginning with lower scores focus on what you have rather than what you lack. So ask yourself these questions:

- What is it that has helped me get from zero to where I am now? (If it is zero, what's helped me to get out of minus figures?)
- What is it that tells me that I am at this point and not at zero?
- What am I doing that I could do a bit more of to increase my satisfaction?
- What do I imagine will be happening for me one point up the scale?
- What represents good enough for me and how will I know I am there?
- How will I know when I've reached a ten?

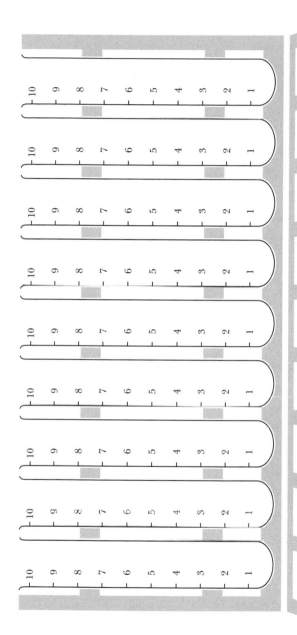

Life satisfaction analysis

Now, repeat the process for your mid-range scores and then your higher scores. Each time emphasize the positives – that is, what you have already.

So with these new insights, let's carry out another personal experiment.

Personal experiment: uplifts

Using the results from the life analysis exercise, choose three areas in your life that you have given the lowest satisfaction scores. This is what we will work on for a week to create daily uplifts. So, based on what you already know brings you satisfaction in these life areas, consider:

• What small things can you imagine doing (each day) over the next week that you think would take you one point higher up the scale?

Write each of these life areas as column headings and then list three actions for each.

Life area 1	Life area 2	Life area 3
Action 1	Action 1	Action 1
Action 2	Action 2	Action 2
Action 3	Action 3	Action 3

Now, focusing on each of the life areas, which of your suggestions would you be prepared to try out over the next week as a personal experiment? Remember, you're just collecting information (insight) so there's no possibility of failure. Either way you get a result (valuable feedback).

- Practice using the SMARTER criteria to make sure that your goal is *Specific*, *Measurable*, *Achievable*, *Realistic*, *Time-bound* (that is, one week), *Enthusiastic* (and positively worded), and *Reviewed*.
- At the end of the week, rate your satisfaction in each of the life areas to assess the difference (on a scale of zero to ten).
- If it hasn't made much of an impact, assess what else has been going on that week that may have detracted from your satisfaction (i.e. review).
- Alternatively, set yourself a slightly bigger goal for the following week and repeat the experiment.

This structured approach can be used to help maintain a commitment to daily/weekly uplifts and will help enhance your overall feel for the day/week, thus increasing your life satisfaction ratings. It's a matter of focussing on the good stuff. Ideally, try this method for four weeks and at the end of that period look at all of your ratings. Remember, the Pareto Principle states that 20% of what we do yields 80% of the results. Use this method and you will begin to discover your 'magical' 20%.

Now let's consider different types of goals, before moving on to tools and techniques for managing longer-term goals.

Doing, getting and being

Our goals really boil down into three main types:

1   What we want to do (doing),
2   What we want to have or get (getting), and
3   What we want to be (being).

Doing goals

Doing goals are the action-oriented or performance goals. These include participating in hobbies or sporting activities, doing more of what you enjoy, or giving a public speech or presentation – perhaps travelling, going on holiday, or the more day-to-day things like showing affection to one's partner, doing the filing, the ironing and so on. Doing goals can also be more far-reaching. They can be about taking action to meet your values.

> What are your *doing* goals?

Getting goals

Getting goals (having goals) are about things that we would like to have. These can include having a family, pursuing a successful career, a loving relationship, good sex life and so on. These goals are frequently emotionally motivated, but can equally be about esteem or ego, with an emphasis on the material world. These might include things like a new car, a big house, designer clothes and so on.

> What are your *getting* or *having* goals?

Being goals

Being goals focus on personal aspirations, that is, ideally how we would like to be – a more effective parent, a better communicator, listener, lover and so on. These goals may also relate to specific situations, such as being more confident in the workplace. These goals are somewhat difficult to quantify. What exactly does 'better' mean? Clearly, the emphasis is on process rather than absolute outcome. So, it is important to be able to translate these goals into actions, i.e. into a number of doing goals. What concrete actions constitute being 'better'? The zero to ten scale – and accompanying questions – are particularly useful to help measure the before- and after-effects of taking action.

> What are your *being* goals?

Maintenance goals

It is also crucial to set maintenance goals for our strengths. For instance, I consider that I have good communication skills. However, I was not born a good at communicator. In fact, as a child I had a mild stammer (stutter), mainly when I became anxious. The thing I feared more than anything was reading out loud to the class. It's something I had to work at – especially as my preferred career end-state involves doing what I dreaded most in school. Furthermore, I still attend seminars and workshops to maintain those skills, even now. Maintenance goals are about recognizing that skill acquisition is an ongoing process. It's like the phrase 'use it or lose it'. Athletes and musicians keep doing what they are good at, so they stay good!

So ask yourself these questions:

1 What am I good at?
2 What are my core skills?
3 How did I get good at those things? What did I do?
4 What am I doing to make sure those skills stay sharp?
5 What opportunities are there to practice those skills?
6 What opportunities are there to stretch those skills?
7 What goals can I set to help maintain and develop my strengths?

By analysing what you are good at and how you got good at it, you will see patterns and strategies emerge. Also, you may be able to transfer your success strategy to other goals. We don't get good at things by chance; we work at them. To keep in 'tip-top' shape we need to maintain that edge and set those maintenance goals. You can use the life analysis (test tube) chart for this, and instead focus on your high scores. Ask yourself, what you need to do this week (or month) to maintain that satisfaction rating.

This takes us to the subject of longer-term goals.

LONG RANGE FORECASTS

So far we have been looking at making a difference with the small stuff – short-term goals. However, the work we did in Chapter Three on values suggests a longer-term view. In this section we consider goals that may take us further up the life satisfaction scale.

So what are your goals for six months, a year, three years and five years from now? What are your preferred end-states? Let's return to the various life areas used earlier for the life satisfaction analysis:

Health/well-being	Intimacy	Fun/leisure	Personal development
Wealth/finances	Vocation	Support network	Supporting strengths
Home/environment	Spirituality	Relaxation	Supporting values

I've also added two categories of supporting strengths and values. You may wish to add your own life areas.

Now, pick three areas to work on and put them as headings in the following table.

1	2	3
Three to six months goal:	Three to six months goal:	Three to six months goal:
One year goal:	One year goal:	One year goal:
Three to five years goal:	Three to five years goal:	Three to five years goal:

Now choose one of those goals and break it down into milestones. I have used six in the following box, but it can be as many as you like:

MILESTONES (SUB-GOALS)					
1	2	3	4	5	6
When?	*When?*	*When?*	*When?*	*When?*	*When?*

Now ⟵——————————————⟶ *Preferred end-state*

Each of these milestones can be treated as sub-goals. Ideally, make the sub-goals doable but slightly challenging. This helps to build motivation as you experience a continual sense of achievement. It builds confidence too.

Use this process for all of your major (longer-term) goals. It doesn't matter if you don't get it exactly right first time. Goal setting is an ongoing process not a one-shot deal!

In the next section we consider tools and techniques for creating compelling action plans.

On par, go flow and grow

In golf, every hole is classified by its par. It is the theoretical number of strokes that expert golfers should require for getting the ball into the hole. For goal setting I give you PAR which refers to:

- Plan,
- Action, and
- Result (or Review).

Using PAR for the basis of all goal setting, if the action doesn't immediately lead to the desired result, this offers an opportunity to reflect and go back to the planning stage as in the learning cycle (Chapter Two).

The use of a formula in the form of an acronym (string of letters) for memory aids has become very popular in goal setting. They help to keep us focused on that all-important, well-formed outcome. Earlier we discussed SMARTER goals as a way of ensuring a tighter definition. Perhaps the most famous goal-setting acronym is the GROW model. Originally a model in psychotherapy it has since been adapted and popularized by John Whitmore. GROW stands for:

- **G**oal – analysed and stated using the SMARTER criteria.
- **R**eality – check your existing circumstances, your opportunities and obstacles.
- **O**ptions – consider a number of options of achieving the goal.
- **W**ill/Wrap-up – as in I *will* chose this one and I will wrap this up.

My modification of GROW is GO-FLOW, which serves to remind us that goals can help create a state of flow as opposed to just 'going with the flow'. A blank form can be found in the appendices. GO-FLOW stands for:

- **G**oal – started and analysed using the SMARTER criteria.
- **O**bservation – observing opportunities, reality and choices.
- **F**eelings – checking your feelings, perceptions, emotions and attitudes to the goal.
- **L**imitations or let-downs – considering what the limitations are for this goal, how you can counter them and how you will deal with let-downs.
- **O**ptions – considering all possible options of achieving the same outcome.
- **W**ill – I will do it.

A useful technique to use with GO-FLOW is SWOT analysis.

SWOT
SWOT stands for: *Strengths, Weaknesses, Opportunities,* and *Threats.* It is a useful technique for supporting goal setting.

- *Strengths.* What's pushing me forward? What are my strengths and how can I best use them to attain my goals? What skills and expertise do I have? What advantages do I have? (It's often useful to consider things from someone else's perspective as well as your own.) What do other people see as my strengths?

- *Weaknesses.* What's holding me back? What are my weaknesses that hinder goal achievement? How best can I manage them? What skills and expertise do I lack? What could I improve on and what should I avoid? What things are people around me likely to see as my weaknesses? Do other people perceive weaknesses that I don't see?
- *Opportunities.* What's clearing the way? What are the (external) opportunities, resources and choices are available to me to support my goals? How can I maximize these opportunities? Consider these also in the context of your strengths: do they open up opportunities for me? Also, look at your weaknesses and ask yourself: could I open up opportunities for managing or minimizing my weaknesses?
- *Threats.* What's getting in the way? What are the (external) threats to achieving my goal? How can I defend against them or minimize them? What are people around me doing? What threats might my weaknesses expose me to? How might my strengths ward off threats?

Taken together, these tools can help create watertight action plans. Whereas SMARTER focuses on goal definition, PAR, GROW and GO-FLOW emphasize the importance of the planning process. SWOT offers an opportunity to focus on strengths and opportunities and anticipate (and minimize) weaknesses and threats.

Using the heat-seeking missile analogy, we can see that the well-defined approach helps program more accurate co-ordinates, ensuring that we stay focused on out target.

For those of you who are not keen on acronyms we will now return to the topic of motivation, which is an acronym-free zone.

Motivation

It is vitally important to have a strong sense of ownership of our goals. We need to perceive them as worthwhile – that is, in support of our values – if we are to take and maintain action in pursuit of them. Goals need to be rewarding (positive reinforcement – see Chapter Two) or help us move away from unpleasant consequences (negative reinforcement – see Chapter Two). Personally owned goals intrinsically have a stronger pull than the goals we are doing for others or because of situational demands (such as some work-related goals).

Our motivations represent the fuel in the ship's engine room. Our values and strengths are like renewable energy sources. They are our *internal motivators*, our *internal positive reinforcement*. They provide built-in rewards. By contrast, *external motivators* (often material rewards) still provide reinforcement but are fleeting or not a constant or reliable source. So, for instance, we can gain self-esteem by setting goals in line with our values that stretch us. Alternatively, we can buy a designer jacket. That will also boost our esteem for a while. However, it's a form of esteem that will fade or wear out. Also, what if we are only motivated by external sources and the supply runs out? What happens when the money runs our or the pats on the back cease? Do we then cease to reach for our goals? An over-reliance on external sources of motivation can lead to dependence on them. Of course, it's possible to use both types of motivator, but it's important to be aware of the differences.

This simple exercise will help to clarify your motivations. Think of a goal you would like to achieve and this time make it a slightly longer-term goal, say between one and three months. Using the following table, in the first column, come up with ten positive benefits of achieving this goal. In the second column think of ten disadvantages (negative consequences) of *not* achieving it. Do not be concerned how big or small the reasons are, just come up with ten of each. You may use a separate sheet of paper divided into two columns if you prefer.

My goal is:	
The positive benefits of achieving this goal	The negative consequences of *not* achieving this goal
1	1
2	2
3	3
4	4
5	5
6	6
7	7
8	8
9	9
10	10

This list provides a motivational double-whammy, with a clear idea of ebb and flow – that is, what the goals take you towards and what they move you away from. It is a good idea to regularly review your list of motivators, adding to it if you wish, to maintain your overall motivation. Wherever possible relate these motivations to your values. Here are two questioning techniques that will help you do this: *follower* and *leader* *questions.*

Followers and leaders

In every courtroom drama on television we hear the words 'Objection. Leading the witness'. Leading questions are phrased in order to get the desired answer. However, they aren't much use if you don't know what you desire. One way to explore your desires and values is to use 'leader' questions and 'follower' questions. Both help you to explore what is at the heart of your wishes (goals). Essentially the same question is repeated, each time updating the next question with the previous insight.

Leader question

Leader questions help us to strip away the layers to reveal the terminal values that underpin both our goals and our external motivators.

Ask yourself:

1   What will achieving <goal> do for me?
2   What will <answer to previous question> do for me?
3   Repeat question 2 until you feel you have exhausted the possible answers.

Here's an example:

Q   What will <passing my driving test> do for me?
A   I will be able to buy a car.
Q   What will <buying a car> do for me?
A   It will mean no more waiting for buses.
Q   What will <no more waiting for buses> do for me?
A   I will have more time and not have to rush.
Q   What will <having more time and not having to rush> do
     for me?
A   I will be more relaxed.
Q   What will <being more relaxed> do for me?
A   I will be happier.

In this case, passing a driving test boils down to the terminal value of happiness – the ultimate preferred end-state. Of course, this line of questioning may have taken many different directions. So, for others, passing a driving test may have brought a feeling of significance, or any other value.

Once we have uncovered the terminal value, we can then ask: How else could I achieve this value? What other goals would lead to happiness or significance? Using this technique can help generate alternative opportunities and choices to meet the same value.

The accompanying technique is designed to uncover the (psychological) blocks and obstacles preventing us from making progress on goal attainment.

Follower question
This technique follows the same repeated pattern as the leader question technique:

Ask yourself:

1 What stops me from <goal>?
2 And what stops me from <answer>?
3 As before, repeat question 2 until you feel you have exhausted the possible answers.

Here's an example:

Q What stops me from <doing that huge pile of ironing or paperwork>?
A I'm not in the mood.
Q And what stops me from <being in the mood>?
A It's just such a big job. I don't know where to start.
Q And what stops me from <knowing where to start>?
A No bloody system in place.
Q And what stops you from having <a bloody system in place>?
A Er me, I suppose. I'd never thought about it before.
Q And what stops you from <thinking about it now>?
A Nothing. If I could come up with a system so the task didn't seem so huge then maybe I'd feel more inclined to do it.

The follower question technique is designed to strip away negative attitudes and psychological resistance to getting started on a goal. In effect, it helps create a shift in our perceptual set.

So, let's put together all of the ideas from this chapter to create a compelling action plan. A blank form can be found in the appendix.

GOALS ACTION PLAN: STEP BY STEP

1 Start with an area of your life for your goal setting.
2 Write out your goal. You don't have to get it perfect the first time.
3 Now put your goal in the SMARTER format. You may wish to get a large sheet of paper and divide it up into six sections for each of the SMARTER criteria.
4 Apply GROW or GO-FLOW, and SWOT.
5 Now write down at least three to five reasons for wanting to achieve that goal.
6 Rate your commitment to attaining this goal on a scale of one to ten. Ten equals 'totally committed' and one equals 'only slightly committed'.
7 What makes it this rating? What have you done to get it up to this number?
8 What do you imagine would need to be going on for your commitment rating to be higher?
9 Take another sheet of paper and divide it into two columns. In the left-hand column make a list of all the obstacles that might prevent you from achieving your goal.
10 Now in the right-hand column write down next to each obstacle what you could do to overcome it. You may draw on existing resources or enlist the help of others. You may also consider seeking out new resources and solutions.
11 Break your main goal down into a series of sub-goals, each with its own target date. As you achieve the sub-goals, ticking them off will help to maintain your motivation.
12 Set an overall target date for your goal.
13 If at any time you find you are not running to schedule, take remedial action and if necessary adjust the target dates for your sub-goals. If you get stuck at one place, ask

yourself whether there is anything else you could be getting on with. Adjust the target date if necessary.

14 Finally, decide how you are going to celebrate when you have achieved the goal.

So, there you have all the tools and techniques for creating compelling action plans.

GOALS FOR GOALS SAKE?

The goal-oriented approach to personal and professional development is not without its critics. Some may argue that a life spent goal chasing can mean a life always focused in the future and never in the present. The result, it is argued, is a lack of contentment, always hankering after the next goal fix, but never taking time to enjoy it. Of course this may well be the case if we only chase goals that are set by other people. However, if we set our own goals that play to our strengths, meet our values and put us into flow, then we will surely experience contentment. It is also important to find a way to make time to celebrate your achievements and regularly take stock. Yes, that's right, you can set celebration goals too!

Despite our best intentions, for most of us, New Year's resolutions rarely last. It's easy to change for a while, but without well-defined (SMARTER) goals that are in keeping with your personal values, without motivation, without a strategy for dealing with obstacles and disappointments and without action, best intentions fizzle out and remain wishful thinking. You can read a thousand self-help books but if you still have none of these things then all you've really done is invest in another space-filler for the bookshelf. Now that's not my preferred end-state for this book and I hope it's not yours either.

Remember that the accurate evaluation (insight) and persistent application of feedback (ownership and action) are the keys to goal attainment. Do this and you will enjoy those preferred end-states and positive lasting changes you desire.

DRYING OFF

Review: From the familiar experience of New Year's resolutions we have used these insights to ponder the subject of goal setting – from attitudes to tried-and-tested tools and techniques for creating watertight action plans. Addressing the subject of life-balance, motivation, and matching goals to values are crucial factors in goal-setting success. Playing to our strengths and setting goals that extend our reach can even bring about an increased sense of happiness.

In the next chapter we will ponder how the strategic use of the innate power of imagination can help support the pursuit of our personal preferred end-states.

REFLECTION (*REFL-ACTION*)

1   **INSIGHT**: What are the three most important things
     you learned in this chapter?

(i)

(ii)

(iii)

2   **OWNERSHIP**: What impact has this had in terms of
     the way you think about your accountability for your
     life and goals?

3   **ACTION**: What action does this inspire you to take
     to make a positive change in your life? What personal
     experiment might you conduct to get feedback and in-
     sight?

Chapter Seven

ALL THAT YOU EVER IMAGINED IT WOULD BE ...

Creative visualization, imagery and mental rehearsal

There are more things in heaven and earth, Horatio, than are dreamt of in your philosophy.

William Shakespeare

You cannot depend on your eyes when your imagination is out of focus.

Mark Twain

We lift ourselves by our thought, we climb upon our vision of ourselves. If you want to enlarge your life, you must first enlarge your thought of it and of yourself.

Orison Swett Marden

DIPPING A TOE
Preview: In this chapter, we'll ponder the strategic use of the imagination for personal development goals.

IMAGINE THAT!

Imagination is a fundamental part of being human. It's not a gift bestowed on the chosen few. Just like every other aspect of human psychology, it is not an all-or-nothing process. We all have it to varying degrees.

We use imagination every time we worry, exaggerate or refuse to walk under a ladder. Watching a TV cookery show and finding your mouth watering at the food requires imagination. Reading a book, being scared of the dark or daydreaming all require imagination. So, seeing as we all have it, this chapter is about how we can use it to support our personal development.

Our brains and bodies do not easily distinguish between reality and fantasy – that is why we can be moved to tears, scared or sexually aroused simply by reading words on the printed page. We conjure up the mental images and our brain responds as if they were real experiences. In this chapter we exploit this 'loophole' with various techniques to tap strategically into our imagination. This tactical use of our imagination to create mental images builds on the relaxation exercises covered in Chapter Six, and takes direction from your goal setting from the previous chapter. The visualization and imagery techniques in this chapter can be learned by anyone and offer a masterclass in advanced relaxation and perceptual filtering to support our goals.

However, before we discuss the background to visualization techniques, let's briefly consider the terminology.

Terminology

There are a number of terms for techniques that strategically use the imagination; these include *creative visualization, imagery, mental rehearsal, manifesting* and *cosmic ordering.* The latter two are New Age spin-offs of visualization techniques. Both have a quasi-spiritual emphasis and appeal to people with an external locus of control (see Chapter Five) in their lives, that is, low on ownership and low on action. The difference here is that we consider how to use imagination and visualization to *support* (active) goal setting, *not* to replace it.

Creative visualization

This is perhaps the most frequently used term for the strategic use of the imagination. Visualization is act of forming mental images, and the creative bit involves using your imagination to change them. For instance, picture a boat. That's visualization. Imagine painting the boat a different colour (that's creative visualization). The term is off-putting for some people as it implies an aptitude for forming mental images. As discussed in Chapter Four, your sense preference might not be visual. However, most people can improve their visualization skills to be good enough. We'll consider a simple and fun exercise later in the chapter.

Imagery

This term arose from the criticism of an overemphasis on visual skills. Although imagery still strongly implies a visual preference it also offers scope for the other senses. This means that we don't have to create a picture of something, just a *sense* of it, which may comprise sounds, sensations and feelings. We can focus on our preferred senses (Chapter Four) to create images that are personally more compelling.

Imagery and visualization are used interchangeably in this chapter.

Mental rehearsal

As its name implies, mental rehearsal has an emphasis on process and action. It involves creating mental motion pictures of you in particular situations actually doing something. It is based in the old adage that says 'practice makes perfect'. As our brains find it difficult to distinguish between reality and imagination, skills practised mentally have similar beneficial effects to practice in the real world. It may sound fantastical, but top athletes use it to help perfect their skills. Essentially it works at the level of developing schemas and programming our perceptual filters.

ADVANCED PERCEPTUAL FILTERING

From a psychological perspective, the use of visualization techniques follows from the idea that we are defined by what we focus on. Actively and strategically we retune our perceptual filters to positive outcomes, using pictures, sounds and other sensations. To realize our goals we need to do more than create a mental picture and wait for the returns. They offer a way forward to support the principles of *insight, ownership* and *action*, not a way out. Think visualiz-*action*; not 'visual-eyes-closed and hope for the best'!

Visualization-type techniques are used in sports psychology to enhance performance, in personal development coaching and various types of psychotherapy. Essentially, the techniques work on the principles of conditioning discussed in Chapter Two. Working with the learning cycle, changes are created in our perceptual filters and indeed also in our schemas. In effect, the techniques help to reprogramme our personal perceptual software. Visualization also forms a large part of *Neuro-Linguistic Programming* (NLP). NLP is a collection of techniques, with a practical emphasis, distilled from psychotherapy and early self-help material. Many of the techniques are very useful, but the bold claims of *instant* change from some NLP practitioners are not supported by research evidence. Change usually occurs in line with the psychological principles of learning as outlined in this book and, of course, when the person wants to change (ownership).

Many people are unaware that they use visualization techniques routinely, every time they worry. So, since we all know how to worry, it makes sense to transform this existing skill into a strength.

POSITIVE WORRYING
What if – if only

We all worry at some time during our lives. Some people excel at it. Whenever we worry, we imaginatively create and rehearse the worst! It is a process by which we replay images of past events (if only), reliving them over and over. We can even worry about things that have not yet happened and create images of future events (what if) and play them over and over in our heads. This means we have all had plenty of visualization practice. It's just a matter of adapting it for a use that is more productive. 'What if' and 'if only' may also be viewed as questions of possibility. From this perspective, visualization is just *positive worrying*. It's just a matter of tuning in to what we want to move towards (goals and values) by switching imagined negative outcomes for positive ones.

The placebo effect

Worrying can take its toll on us physically. We often talk about worrying ourselves sick. The links between stress, worry and ill-health are well documented. However, so too are the links between relaxation and wellness. Mere thoughts and images can bring about physical and psychological changes. So, just as mental images can have detrimental effects, they can also be deployed for positive effect. Used in conjunction with traditional Western medicine, studies have confirmed a beneficial effect of visualization and relaxation techniques. One theory is that they help to trigger the natural placebo response. A placebo is a sugar pill used as part of the controlled clinical trials for new medicines. Despite containing no active medicinal ingredients a significant number of patients receiving sugar pills show an improvement in their medical conditions. People believe they are taking medicine which they expect to have a beneficial effect, and it does. We still don't fully understand the placebo effect but it indicates strongly that the mind (imagination) can be used to impressive effect. Increasingly, visualization techniques are being used side-by-side with traditional Western medicine, especially in medical complaints with a stress component, such as cancer (see Further Reading for more details).

Peak performance

We're told that practice makes perfect. This is true. However, not all of this practice needs to be in the real world. Practising in the imagination has a performance-enhancing effect too. For instance, a study has shown that basketball players who practised shooting hoops in their imagination demonstrated almost as much improvement in accuracy as those who did so in real life. Similar findings have been found for other sports, and visualization techniques have become a principal tool in the quest for peak performance amongst top athletes including golfers, footballers and bodybuilders. As a result, these techniques are used in the world of work. They can even be used to help with the humble driving test, rather like your own personal driving simulator.

So, if you've gained the insight and taken ownership, but hesitate to take action, you can first try things out in your imagination before trying it out in the real world. You can then take the feedback and changes and make the necessary adjustments in your head before trying them out in the real world. Let's experiment with this idea.

TWO PERSONAL EXPERIMENTS IN VISUALIZATION
Building on the relaxation exercises covered in Chapter Five, both of the following techniques allow you to use all of your senses in creating the imaginative experiences and are based on familiar real-life events.

1 Morning glory
Morning glory is an experiment is energizing visualization. It doesn't require any additional time to do it. As soon as you leap out of bed in the morning following your Rise and Shine Breathing Exercise (Chapter Five), head for the shower. As you stand under the water, imagine a beautiful healing, refreshing, invigorating light streaming from the showerhead (as well as the water). The light may be white, pink, golden or pale blue: you choose. Imagine this light-charged energy washing away the tiredness and charging you up for the day. Use whatever positive thought you wish. Do this everyday for two weeks, or more if you wish. What effect does it have on you? You may also wish to repeat the process before going to bed.

However, why wait for a real shower? If you wish to try this experiment now, use your imagination to create the whole experience. Read the following instructions a few times and then try it out.

1 Get comfortable, close your eyes and perform ten deep abdominal breaths.
2 Count down from ten to one on the exhalation of each breath.
3 Imagine that you are just stepping into the shower and the water is the perfect temperature. How does the water feel against your body? What does it sound like?
4 Imagine the water is charged with a positive, cleansing and invigorating light (plus any other positive qualities you wish to invest it with).
5 Feel the light-charged water empowering you, from the outside in.
6 Imagine your whole body lights up with this positive healing energy.
7 All of your fears and worries are bathed in the light and washed away. Imagine them flowing down the plughole. Smile as you see them spiralling away.
8 As you breathe in, feel the light grow brighter and brighter with you. Imagine it extends outside of your body so that you are totally enveloped in light.
9 Enjoy this feeling for a moment.
10 Now draw this energy inside you and know that you can call upon it any time you wish.
11 Smile and count from one to ten, knowing that when you reach ten you will be alert, refreshed and energized.
12 Do this everyday for a week or two or three.

As with all of the personal experiments the aim is simply to try things out to see how they work for you. Then, reflect and adjust your approach until you have something that works for you.

The second personal experiment also works well as a meditation and involves taking a familiar experience and exaggerating it for an improved relaxation effect.

2 My sanctuary

Many commercial relaxation tapes use guided imagery to help listeners to induce their relaxation responses. Against a background of 'floaty flutey' music a soothing voice narrates an ideal scene that might include water, beaches, meadows, clouds and other symbols of tranquillity. The trouble is that one person's idea of paradise might be another person's package tour cliché. The process is more effective when you are able to create your own relaxing scenes.

Preparation
For this experiment consider the most relaxing environment you have ever experienced (or can imagine).

Technique
1 Induce your relaxation response with some long, deep abdominal breaths.
2 Now begin to picture your ideal place of relaxation.
3 Focus on the sights, sounds, smells and other sensations.
4 Think about your emotions at the time. How were you feeling?
5 Imagine those sensations occurring in your body now.

6   Keep adding detail to make the experience more vivid, more compelling.
7   Really act into the experience. Exaggerate.
8   Keep adding details until you feel as if you're there.
9   Enjoy the experience.

Variations

A   You may have more than one ideal place. Instead, use your imagination to create a blend. Take the best elements from your ideal places to create a 'super-paradise'.
B   Why limit yourself to places you have been. You might include places that you've only heard of or seen in pictures. Take the elements that appeal to you and create your perfect idea of a sanctuary to which you can escape whenever you please.
C   Let your imagination take over totally and create anything you wish. The only criterion is that the place represents supreme relaxation for you.

Whatever the content of your ideal place, the aim is to create a special sanctuary as vividly as possible. What better way to get to sleep at night than by going to your place of sanctuary? Try this every night for two weeks and note the effects it has on your day-to-day living.

Now let's consider a technique designed to help explore and improve your creative abilities. Often, we don't know what our limitations are until we actually test the boundaries. Just treat the exercise as a personal experiment and assess the feedback.

IMAGINATION WORKOUTS

We all have the ability to creatively visualize to varying degrees. Every time we recognize a face, in part, we are using visualization. Picture the face of a female friend (visualize). Now give her an enormous handlebar moustache. That's imagination (the creative aspect). A student on one of my courses claimed not to be able to visualize. I asked her *not* to picture a pink elephant. I then asked her if she had in fact done the opposite and pictured a pink elephant. I was somewhat surprised when she said 'no'. To prove me wrong she had deliberately pictured a blue whale. Nevertheless, she had created a mental image of something. It's important not to get hung up about the extent of your visualizing ability. You don't have to be an Olympic creative visualizer! If you've ever worried, laughed at a joke or experienced an emotion while reading a book or watching TV, then that's good enough. A vague image focused on persistently is better than a sharp image held fleetingly. You can also work with your preferred sense (Chapter Four) to help compose the image too.

These simple exercises provide effective ways of exploring and boosting your creative visualization abilities. As before, try them out like experiments and don't forget to have fun with them.

1 Taking shape

Among the first things we learn to draw, as children, are simple shapes such as circles, squares and triangles. So let's begin our visualization workout with these:

- Get a piece of paper and draw a large shape in the centre of it.
- Make it big, bold and ideally brightly coloured.

- Now spend a few minutes concentrating on it. Really scrutinize it.
- When you think you've got it firmly imprinted in your mind then close your eyes and attempt to create a mental picture of it.
- Trace the outline of this shape in your mind.
- If it's just a vague sense of the shape then that's a good start.
- You can open your eyes to refresh your memory and try again.

This is basically all we mean by visualization. It's the ability to recreate a mental image (however fuzzy or sketchy it may be). The creative part – the imagination – comes when we attempt to change it. To do this, close your eyes and create the image of the simple shape again.

- Now bring the image closer to you. Allow it to get bigger.
- Now take it further away from you and allow it to get smaller.
- Bring it back to its original size and imagine that someone has kicked it and see it changing shape. Visualize a dent in the shape.
- Imagine that it gets a few kicks and its outline becomes wavy.
- Now imagine that it changes colour.
- Allow it to flash between different colours.
- Now change it into another shape.

All of this is imagination and we are all able to do it to varying degrees. I'd say don't worry if you don't feel your pictures are vivid enough. But, if you are worrying, you are using imagination. You are comparing what you are getting to what you think it should look like. This requires imagination. So, just relax and work with what you've got. It's good enough already.

Now that you've achieved some success with basic shapes, you can experiment with simple drawings such as a house, a car or a vase of flowers using the same process.

Let's now take this a step further.

2 Fruit of your imagination

Having developed your skills with two-dimensional objects, let's now work with some everyday three-dimensional items: fruit.

I reckon this is a good topic seeing as we're supposed to have five portions of fruit and vegetables every day, and so they should be readily at hand. So here goes:

- Take a piece of fruit, an apple, a pear or a peach – something that's easy to bite into. Yes I know that pomegranates are good for us, but they are so fiddly.
- Hold the piece of fruit in front of you and, as before, really scrutinize it. Notice the contours and imperfections. Hold it very close and get an idea of the detail.
- Now hold it at arms length and keep focused on it.
- When you think it's imprinted in your mind, close your eyes and recreate an image of it.
- You may want to open your eyes again and refresh your memory. Go back and forth a few times.
- Again, recreating an image is visualization. Now let's get creative.
- Close your eyes and imagine taking a bite from it. It's juicy and sweet. Taste it.
- In your imagination, hold the fruit away from you and see the bite mark.

- Still with your eyes closed, in your imagination, bring it back to your mouth and take another bite. Again taste the juice and the sweetness.
- Now imagine the fruit spinning in the air with two bites out of it.
- Now imagine the fruit floating in the air in front of you.
- Bring it closer. Now take it further away.
- Now turn it blue. Now change it back.
- Now change it into a different piece of fruit.

You may even have noticed whilst doing this that it made your mouth water. Try it again with a lemon. In your imagination, cut it in half and inhale that sharp citrus fragrance. Bite into it. Is your mouth watering now? So you can see how it is possible to create a physical response from a mental image.

This is the skill that we will be developing and working with to support out goals. So, let's take the imagination training a step further.

3   The peg-word system

Originally a memory improvement technique, the peg-word system is a useful tool to help develop the imaginative aspect of creative visualization. It involves pairing each of the numbers from one to ten with an object. To make it easier, each pair (number and object) rhyme. Although primarily a visual technique it is even more effective if you add detail from all senses such as sounds and smells.

The number/object pairs are:

1   *One goes with bun* – so picture a big, sticky, iced bun with a cherry on the top, or any other bun that takes your fancy. It might be someone's great buns you're picturing!

2 *Two goes with shoe* – so picture a shoe. It can be your favourite, battered old shoe or your favourite designer shoe. It can even be Dorothy's ruby slipper from *The Wizard of Oz*.

3 *Three goes with tree* – picture of any tree you like. It can be a young sapling, a sturdy oak, a fruit tree or one full of blossom.

4 *Four goes with door* – you may picture your own front door, the door to your office or a door to a famous building you've visited. Any door will do as long as you try to create a strong mental image of it.

5 *Five goes with hive* – picture a beehive with bees buzzing around. Of course, you could also picture the old, beehive hairstyle.

6 *Six goes with sticks* – this can be the image of sticks lying in the forest, chopsticks, hockey sticks, drumsticks or playing pooh sticks. Any old sticks will do.

7 *Seven goes with heaven* (or Devon if you live in England) – whatever your view of heaven is, create a picture of it.

8 *Eight goes with gate* – it can be your garden gate, something grand and ornate, or the gate to a farm you've visited.

9 *Nine goes with swine* – picture a pig. It can be a pig at a farm or a cartoon pig. Make it big. Hear the grunting and smell the sty!

10 *Ten goes with hen* – picture a big fat cartoon hen, or a hen that you saw at the local farm.

Goes through these a few times and also repeat the rhyming-pairs list out loud:

one–bun, two–shoe, three–tree, four–door, five–hive, six–sticks, seven–heaven, eight–gate, nine–swine, ten–hen.

Repetition will imprint it firmly in your memory as this forms the basis of the memory–creativity workout. Close your eyes and as you recite each word pair, let the images form in your mind.

Once you've mastered this, the next stage is to use the peg-word pairs as hooks to remember other things. With a touch of imagination, the system enables you to remember a list of ten items in order. And since there's no better way to learn the technique than actually doing it, here are ten objects for you to remember:

1 Slug
2 Cat
3 Ball
4 Hammer
5 Cake
6 Bread
7 Pink Cadillac
8 Sock
9 Wig
10 Football

I will guide you through the technique. So, for each of the numbered items in the list, you need to link it to its corresponding peg word and create a picture of it, something like this:

1 *Bun and slug*: Imagine a big slimy slug crawling all across your lovely iced bun. In fact, that's probably not icing at all! Gross but fun!

2 *Shoe and cat:* Imagine a cute cat in rather elegant red stiletto heel shoes. Alternatively, imagine the cat with one paw in the shoe trying to walk and tripping over. Imagine your cat using your favourite shoes as its lavatory!

3 *Tree and ball:* Imagine a ball stuck up a tree. It's not the most original image but as long as it links the two items together it doesn't matter. I'm thinking a beach ball here, but any kind of ball will do!

4 *Door and hammer:* Imagine a huge hammer knocking the door down. It could also be a door with a big hammer instead of a knocker.

5 *Hive and cake:* Imagine the cake on top of a hive, drizzled with honey with bees buzzing around it. Maybe it's a honey-drenched cake in the shape of a hive, with marzipan bees.

6 *Sticks and bread:* Imagine a big loaf of bread with two drumsticks in mid-air, beating out a rhythm on the loaf. Hey! Bread sticks!

7 *Heaven and pink Cadillac:* Imagine the angels driving around in a big shiny pink Cadillac in and out of the gates of heaven, and swerving between the clouds. Assuming of course that is your idea of heaven.

8 *Gate and sock:* It can be as simple as a big sock hanging on a gate to dry, or an old sweaty sock giving off an awful smell.

9 *Swine and wig:* A pig with a wig. It can't get much simpler than that. A big pink pig in big pink wig.

10 *Hen and football:* Imagine a hen laying a football. Imagine the sound it makes. Aaaarrrrrrrgh! Cruel but vivid. I'll leave you to fill in rest of the detail.

Now close the book and shout out (or write down) the items in order. Go for it!

Welcome back.

You may have laboured a little at first but hopefully you remembered most of the list, if not all. The reason why the technique is successful is that it requires us to actively structure our experience. The more work we do, the deeper the memories are encoded. Try this technique out a few times and perhaps enlist the help of someone to test you with ten objects of their choosing. The more you practice the technique, the better you will become. Also, try teaching it to someone else.

Focus on creating big, bright, fun images and add sounds and sensations too – play to your strengths and work with your sense preference (see Chapter Four). You'll find that the more effort you put in to creating a picture, the more impact it has and the more memorable it becomes. Just have fun with it and enjoy the practice. Do it to amuse yourself in the supermarket queue or when waiting for a train or bus.

Now that you have had an imagination workout, let's consider how we can apply creative visualization techniques to the pursuit of your goals, that is, to imagine your preferred personal positive outcomes.

GETTING TO GRIPS WITH GOALS

Anything that has ever been accomplished, from building a ship to making a cocktail, started with a thought and an image. So, the first step in any endeavour is to create a compelling picture of what you wish to move towards. We've been referring to it as a *preferred end-state* or *preferred positive outcome*. It's also often referred to as a *future-desired outcome*.

The GRIP technique brings together the tools and techniques from the previous two chapters, combining goal setting, relaxation and creative visualization. Its four stages are:

1 *Goal* – set a clear, well-defined goal (see Chapter Six).
2 *Relax* – induce your relaxation response (see Chapter Five).
3 *Image* – imagine and visualize an image, bring all of your senses into play (see Chapter Four for sense preference).
4 *Persistence* – focus in on it often.

(i) Goal

The first stage is to set your goal, using processes from the previous chapter – SMARTER, PAR, GROW or GO-FLOW. The aim is to produce that all-important, well-formed outcome. Again, if you have a more substantial goal to achieve, break it down into a number of sub-goals. Then work on each of these in turn.

(ii) Relax

The second stage is to use a relaxation technique (Chapter Five) to induce your relaxation response with any method you desire. If you want to deepen your relaxation then add one of the visualizations such as your ideal place (sanctuary) before proceeding to the third stage.

(iii) Image

In this stage, we create a mental image of the outcome by visualizing the finishing line – that is, the completed goal – your preferred positive outcome. Use preferred senses to add detail to create a vivid, compelling picture. Also, experience the feelings of success and those around you offering congratulations, as if it were really happening. How does it feel? What impact is it having on your body? Create these feelings. If you are taking an examination, then imagine you already have your results in your hand and that you are jumping for joy. Don't concern yourself with how you got there, just focus on your end-point. By creating your images and experiences of your preferred positive outcome and summoning up the emotions that go with success, it gives you a taste of success. It implants the idea in your mind that you have already succeeded. This practice is excellent for helping to build motivation (and confidence).

(iv) Persistence

Persistently tuning in to images of your future desired outcome makes it part of your perceptual filters. So, take advantage of any breaks or quiet times of the day to combine imagery and visualization during your relaxation exercises, and add a few energizing breaths too to create positive physical associations. A relaxed body and mind go together. In Chapter Five we discussed how relaxation is the foundation on which we build confidence.

A key ingredient to maximize the effects of your visualization (imagery) is how you approach it – your attitude. You need to invest in the visualization with a *positive mental attitude*. A half-hearted approach will yield a half-hearted response. You only get back as much as you put in. Boost the effects by suspending your disbelief. Rather than saying to yourself 'Let's see *if* it works', you need to say 'Let's see *how well* it works'. The more you immerse yourself in the process the more effective creative visualization will be for you, keeping your perceptual filters tuned into positive outcomes.

As we have already discussed, imagination can be strategically employed to develop and enhance skills: mental rehearsal. So, let's look at that next.

ALL THAT YOU EVER IMAGINED IT WOULD BE ...

Mental rehearsal

The most accomplished, higher level performers use mental rehearsal to stay at the top of their game. Athletes, artists, pilots, astronauts and surgeons routinely use mental rehearsal to support real-life practice to prepare themselves for challenges. Having already 'seen' and 'experienced' themselves perform flawlessly, it becomes their self-fulfilling prophecy and the resulting performance appears effortless. The process and effects are very much the same whether you want to improve your piano playing, perfect your golf swing, clinch a dance move, practise for your driving test, give a presentation, make a sale or acquire any skill or quality, including improving your confidence. Anyone can practise mental rehearsal in the comfort of their own home. Let's begin by taking a routine task that you already do well, such as making a cup of tea or a sandwich. The process is as follows:

Basic technique

1   Induce your relaxation response by any method you favour. Remember that you can combine techniques to achieve a deeper state of relaxation.
2   Mentally experience yourself performing any task perfectly.
3   Add details from all of your senses to create a vivid and compelling experience.
4   Add the feelings that go with the task, such as anticipating the taste of the cup of tea. Add the reactions of other people as they enjoy the cup of tea and say 'thank you'.
5   Repeat the process with some different scenarios, such as doing your filing or a pile of ironing.

This simple technique allows you to gain the basic skills of mental rehearsal. As before, use your sense preference to make the experience more vivid and compelling. When you are comfortable with the technique, move up to the next level.

Role model remote viewing

For the purposes of this exercise, think of a new skill that you would like to improve, such as your tennis swing, yoga ability, driving skills, presentation skills. Now, think of a role model who excels at your chosen skill, and who you've had some experience of observing in action. You may wish to break the task into component steps and practise each step in turn, before putting the steps together.

So, here's the process:

1 Induce your relaxation response by any method you favour. Remember that you can combine techniques to achieve a deeper state of relaxation.

2 Mentally observe your role model performing the task perfectly.

3 Add details from all of your senses.

4 Once you are satisfied with the experience you are creating, step into the body of your role model, and continue to let them guide your actions.

5 Again, add details from all of your senses to create a vivid and compelling experience.

6 Add the emotions you feel as you perform the task perfectly.

When you are happy with this stage, it's time to ...

Go it alone

1 Induce your relaxation response by any method you favour. Remember that you can combine techniques to achieve a deeper state of relaxation.

2 This time you are performing the task perfectly all on your own.

3 You move your body just as your role model does.

4 Again, add details from all of your senses to create a vivid and compelling experience.

5 Add the emotions you feel as you perform the task perfectly.

Perform your chosen task whenever you get a spare minute, by adding the mental rehearsal to your relaxation practice.

Visualization and imagery techniques are used when we have a clear idea of the preferred outcome – that is, in supporting our goals. However, these techniques can also be used when we don't necessarily know what the outcome should be, such as problem solving. In short, imagery and visualization techniques can help create a shift in our perceptual filters to clear the way to receive solutions. Think of it as possibility programming.

CREATIVE SOLUTION FINDING

We may argue that we're not in the mood or not in the right frame of mind to tackle problems (find solutions). Or maybe we feel as if we've reached a dead end. Once in this mindset, it may be difficult to break free from it. The strategic use of the imagination can help create a shift in these dead-end mindsets.

Have you ever been in a situation when you're stuck? No matter how hard you try you just can't seem to break through. Eventually you just give up and go do something else, such as make a cup of tea or go for a walk. Suddenly, you find that a solution just seems to pop in to your head. It may seem magical, but in psychology it's known as the *incubation* phase of problem solving. I refer to it as 'putting things in my cognitive slow-cooker'. Essentially, our minds will continue to work on the problem if we have put a great deal of effort into the problem, and then switched tasks.

The following three problem-solving techniques are designed to help this psychological phenomenon along. The first technique (*Three Scenes*) helps create a shift to open up your mindset to the possibility of a solution. The second technique (*Team of Advisors*) is used to get a second (perceptual) opinion and the third technique (*Altered States*) simply helps you to change your mood.

(i) Three scenes technique
This is my own version of a basic solution-finding technique distilled from various sources, which my clients have found very useful. The three stages represent the three phases of problem solving: the dilemma, taking action, and the outcome. Ideally you should read the instructions a few times to familiarize yourself with the steps.

Preparation
When you have a problem clearly in mind and have already been attempting to solve it, you are ready to begin. To prepare for the technique, induce your relaxation response using any method you favour.

Step one: The dilemma

1   Visualize the dilemma (problem) and create enough detail to get a real sense of it, but don't dwell on it too much.

2   Project this image in front of you as if it is a hologram, a three-dimensional image in space.

3   Add as much detail as you can from your other senses to create a more vivid image.

4   Now take a deep breath and mentally say the word 'forward' three times.

5   Walk towards the image with a sense of purpose and determination and break straight through it.

6   In your imagination, turn around briefly to see the problem behind you.

7   Know that you have moved forward and have made a breakthrough.

8   Turn back, face straight ahead and take a few long, slow, deep breaths.

9   Repeat 'forward' once more.

Step two: Taking action

1   Create an image of you taking decisive and affirmative action to solve this problem.

2   Experience your sense of determination.

3   It doesn't matter what the action is. It can simply be a symbolic gesture.

4   It may help if you actually use physical gestures to accompany the image.

5   Take a deep breath, and mentally say the word 'resourceful' three times.

6   Now step into that image and become a part of it. Work at summoning up all the feelings that you associate with being resourceful.

7   Take some more deep breaths and mentally repeat 're-sourceful' with increasing emotion.

8   On the horizon you see a shimmering, sparkling dot.

9   Focus on it and give it a welcoming smile.

Step three: The outcome

1   Let the shimmering dot on the horizon become brighter as it moves towards you. It is radiating a beautiful light. You choose the colour.

2   Breathe in the beautiful light, feeling it fully absorbed.

3   Repeat the word 'solution' three times.

4   Just ahead of you a new scene is forming. It is the scene in which you have found the solution to your problem. Imagine someone close to you saying 'well done'.

5   Take a deep breath and step into the scene. Use your energy to make this scene more vivid. How do you feel now that you have succeeded? What are the sights and sounds?

6   Take a deep breath and mentally say the one-word prayer 'success'.

7   Take a few moments to enjoy this feeling and smile or even imagine yourself jumping with joy.

8   Imagine someone takes an instant photograph. Flash. The person hands you the picture. You say 'thank you', look at it and smile again.

9   When you are ready, count yourself back from one to ten.

10 Over the next few days, whenever you have a moment to spare, close your eyes, take a few deep breaths and imag-

ine that final photograph. A solution to your problem will emerge.

Once you have found the solution, you can set about creating an action plan (see Chapter Six), take action and support your endeavours by using the GRIP technique from this chapter.

When we encounter a problem we often seek the opinion of a trusted friend or even go to seek the advice of an expert. However, wouldn't it be great if you could enlist the help of any expert from the past, present or future?

This next exercise helps create a shift in your perceptual filters by considering getting an imaginary second opinion. It is remarkably effective.

(ii) Ship's crew (team of advisors)

When I was studying for my degree, I was working on the statistics for my final year dissertation. I needed help from my supervisor (Dave) but he was on holiday for the next few days. I was sure I couldn't solve the problem and stared at the computer screen in desperation. I sighed deeply then blurted out 'Well how would Dave tackle it if he was here?' I tried to put myself in a Dave-like mindset and then, within minutes, I went right ahead and solved it! I later learned that this approach has appeared in various forms in self-help books. Napoleon Hill referred to it as his 'board of directors', and Jose Silva as his 'laboratory counsellors'. Whatever you decide to call it, the technique of borrowing another's mindset can be a very powerful tool for solution finding.

I have used a version more apt to this book of a Captain on the Bridge with her (or his) crew. I have also offered a more neutral version of consulting room and team of advisors (in brackets). Whenever you need another point of view on a dilemma or decision, this technique will help. Overall it's best if your advisors are people with whom you do not have a strong emotional attachment. Try to think of experts in the field who would give you an objective expert opinion.

As before, read the instructions through a few times before trying it out. The technique has two stages.

Stage one: The bridge

1   Induce your relaxation response by any method you wish.
2   Create a ship's bridge (consulting room) in your imagination. It can be based on something you are familiar with or something totally imagined. It may something quite space-age, like the Star Ship *Enterprise* from *Star Trek*. It can be a boardroom, a study, a library or the dining room. The details are up to you.
3   Spend time adding the detail. You can have an old-fashioned ship's wheel, or a high-tech instrument panel, with a link to the Internet or an Extraterrestrial-Net. You could add a red, velvet chaise longue and an aquarium if you wished. How you decorate it is up to you. The key thing is that it must create a sense of the kind of place where solutions will emerge. Once you have created it, you simply need to recall it next time. Of course you can update (redecorate) it whenever you feel it is necessary.
4   When you are happy with the details of the room, it's time to focus on your dilemma and decision.

Stage two: Your crew

1   When you have a clear sense of your dilemma, sit for a moment and imagine who would be a useful and insightful second-in-command (advisor). It can be anyone from the past or present. It can even be someone from the future – it can be a future 'you' if this helps. Overall, try to focus on objective sources of help.

2   Imagine there is a knock at the door. You walk across the room to welcome your crew (advisors) for a briefing. (Be prepared for anyone to be there. It may be one of the people you have already imagined or it might be someone who takes you by surprise.)

3   Invite your crew in and, when they are all seated, tell them your problem or dilemma. It may just be one or two crew members (advisors) or more. The numbers may vary from time to time.

4   Now go to each one in turn and ask them for their impressions.

5   When they have all offered something, ask each of your crew (advisors) if they have anything to add.

6   Thank your crew (advisors) in turn, because you're a nice kindly Captain (not the one from *Mutiny on the Bounty*), and see them to the door.

7   Take a moment to pause and know that a solution to your problem is beginning to form.

8   Count yourself back from one to ten, knowing that when you reach ten you will be alert and that a solution will follow soon.

9   Repeat the exercise as you feel necessary or if you want to gain further insight.

Although on first impression this technique may seem a little bizarre, it is simply a way of altering your perceptual filters, by thinking yourself into different perspectives – just as I did with my statistics problem. Once a solution emerges for your dilemma, you can press forward and create an action plan to reach the goal and use the GRIP technique to support your actions.

The next technique helps address the problem of not being in the right mood, and helps us to get there, at will.

(iii) Altered states: In the mood

We all have a tendency to want to retell stories of events with a high emotional impact. It may be a hot date, a fantastic holiday, passing your driving test, or singing well at a gig. It can also be traumatic experiences. Retelling the story, you evoke the same emotional response as the experience. You may be moved to tears or to laugh out loud. You may tingle all over, or feel the hairs stand up on the back of your neck. OK, perhaps you didn't wish to be reminded that you have a hairy neck. The point is that you can re-experience good feelings simply by telling and retelling a story.

In Chapter Five we discussed the human ability to induce a relaxation response to help cancel out a stress response. We also routinely talk about 'psyching' ourselves up in the face of a challenging task. All of this points to one thing: we have the ability to change and control our emotional states. This means that you can recreate states of relaxation, feeling energized, confident, resourceful and so on. If you've done it once you can do it again, by talking yourself through the process and evoking other sensations associated with the state, such as body posture. We don't have to passively wait to get into the right mood, we can actively take ourselves there.

Here's a simple technique to help you alter your mental and emotional landscapes when you choose.

Preparation

For the purposes of this technique, think of an emotional state you would like to evoke. It's best to make it a pleasant one and base it on a recent experience. Again, the technique works best when you suspend your disbelief and immerse yourself fully in the experience. Unleash your inner actor. Exaggerate a little. Exaggerate a lot. The more fun you have the better.

Next, pick a trigger word that you want to link with the state. For instance, when I'm facing a challenge, I use the phrase 'let's go'. However, you can simply name the state you want to evoke (resourceful, happy, joyful, energized) or just 'in the mood'!

The technique

1 Induce your relaxation response with ten abdominal breaths, counting down from ten to one.

2 Now, imagine a time when you experienced your chosen emotional state.

3 Recall as much of the detail as you can. What were the sights, sounds and other sensations? How were you feeling at the time? Summon these emotions. Attempt to re-experience the bodily sensations too.

4 Now consider on a scale of zero to ten how real is it? Zero equals not at all, and ten equals 'it's as if I was really there'. Consider what would take you a step higher.

5   If it's a four or a five, what does it need to get you to a six, then a seven? Keep adding more detail from all of your senses. Make the image or experience brighter or less bright, or make the sounds louder or quieter. Use your preferred senses. Use whatever makes it more real for you.

6   What will it take to get it to an eight, nine or even ten? Keep adding the detail and acting into the experience until it's as real and alive as you can make it.

7   Now add your trigger word or phrase (such as, 'let's go') to psych it up even more. Repeat it over and over in your head with increasing emotion, really feel it in your body.

Personal experiment

1   In what mood would you like to start the day? Pick a mood or emotion and follow the *altered states* instructions to get in that mood.

2   Do this every day for a week.

3   Alternatively you can do this every day after lunch to boost your energy levels.

4   What are your observations at the end of the week?

With practice, summoning different emotional states at will will become easier. This is similar to the NLP technique of setting an anchor. To set an anchor, a mental state is recreated much in the way described above. More often, the altered state is linked to a physical gesture, such as a finger tug.

   In the next section we consider a technique that brings together all of the principles learned so far.

GETTING OVER 'IT'

Often, distressing or embarrassing events may return to haunt us. Increasingly they become more vivid every time we replay them. Sometimes we invest in these images the power to prevent us from trying again or moving on. So, the presentation that didn't quite go to plan becomes 'never again'! Even the word 'presentation' seems to evoke your stress response. The more we play negative images, the stronger this aversion becomes. Again, this is a problem of not reflecting on the feedback in order to readjust and try again. However, 'never again' may not be an option, especially if presentations are part of your job.

We've discussed how we can increase the emotional intensity of a mental visualization by turning up the volume and making the image more vivid (and real). This is exactly what we can do with 'haunting' images. So, to lessen the impact, all we need to do is to reverse this process. We need to re-edit the image to take away the vividness and clarity and thus lessen its emotional impact. Here's another personal experiment – the final technique in this chapter – to help you to do just that.

Personal experiment: The director's cut

For this experiment select a mildly negative memory – nothing too traumatic. Try things like a presentation not going to plan or a knock-back from someone you fancied. Once you have something in mind, read these instructions a few times so that you don't have to keep glancing at the book. It's important just to get the idea rather than follow the instructions to the letter.

So try this:

1 Induce your relaxation response by any method you favour.

2 Focus on your negative memory and recall the detail.

3 Rate the intensity of the negative emotions associated with this memory on a scale of one to ten. One means 'mild', ten means 'the most incredibly painful memory you have' and five or six means 'moderately painful'.

4 Notice what you are emphasizing. Is the image up close? If so, does it become less intense if you take it farther away? What's the rating now? Has the intensity reduced?

5 Try projecting the image onto a movie screen and sit a few rows back in the cinema. What's your intensity rating now, on the one to ten scale?

6 How does it feel as you move back a few more rows? How does it feel when you are at the back of the cinema? Check the intensity again.

7 Now imagine that the image turns into a small blurred black and white picture with muffled sound. What's your emotional rating now?

8 Keep running your mental movie and have someone with very 'big' hair sit in front of you partially obscuring your view. How does it feel now?

9 Imagine someone is rustling a crisp packet and slurping their drink and then a mobile phone goes off with one of those ridiculous ring tones. Pick the most inappropriate tune you can think of.

10 Add anything else you can think of to spoil the movie. Maybe someone breaks wind or smuggles a pig into the cinema, or a hairy biker in a tutu starts dancing in the aisle. Use anything your imagination can conjure up to disturb the movie. The more improbable and ridiculous, the better.

11 Now what's the rating on a scale of one to ten? Have you changed the emotional impact?

12 Now begin all over again and run the movie – only this time, play it as you would really like to see it. If it was a presentation make it a great presentation. Create your future desired outcome and use all the techniques to make this a great experience. Add a victorious soundtrack, such as the *Dam Busters* march. There's a list of positive songs in the Further Reading and Resources section.

13 Repeat the whole exercise a few times to condition the new associations.

It's a simple but powerful technique that helps to dull the intensity of a negative experience. It is not necessarily appropriate to treat all memories this way. Some may be deeply significant moments such as the loss of a loved one or the break up of a relationship. The intention is not to trivialize these, so you may just want to do as much as it takes to take the edge off the whole thing. So, for instance, you might move the image further away or change the scene into black and white. Even this small shift may help. In these circumstances it also helps to use *distraction*. In psychology this simply means to occupy your mind with something else, such as learning a new skill. Doing this will make sure that you have less time to rehearse the negative or painful memories.

POSITIVE OUTCOME PROPHECY

All of the material in this chapter is for action rather than mere reflection. It is only possible to gauge the success of these techniques by actually doing them as a series of experiments. Practise them regularly and with enthusiasm, and they help us to become our own *prophets of boom* instead of *profits of doom*. You will also gain a valuable body of evidence as to what works for you. Self-fulfilling prophecies don't have to be negative predictions. The tactical use of our imagination becomes a driving force in helping us to take ownership, retune our filters, focus on solutions and create positive outcome prophecies that come true.

DRYING OFF

Review: In this chapter we pondered the strategic use of the imagination to support personal development goals. We have considered the background to visualization techniques and made connections with other chapters in this book. The tools and techniques in this chapter offer a means of actively retuning your perceptual filters, increasing motivation, problem solving, skills development and even ways to get you in the mood.

In the next chapter we will consider verbal aspects such as how our inner dialogue (the way we talk to ourselves) influences our perceptions and our personal development.

REFLECTION (*REFL-ACTION*)
1 **INSIGHT**: What are the three most important things
you learned in this chapter?

(i)

(ii)

(iii)

2 **OWNERSHIP**: What impact has this had in terms of
the way you think about your accountability for your
life and goals?

3 **ACTION**: What action does this inspire you to take
to make a positive change in your life? What personal
experiment might you conduct to get feedback and insight?

Chapter Eight

WATER WINGS OR CONCRETE GALOSHES?

The power of self-talk

> *Human beings, by changing the inner attitudes of their minds,
> can change the outer aspects of their lives.*
>
> William James
>
> *From without, no wonderful effect is wrought within ourselves,
> unless some interior, responding wonder meets it.*
>
> Herman Melville
>
> *I have learnt silence from the talkative, toleration from the
> intolerant, and kindness from the unkind; yet strange, I am
> ungrateful to these teachers.*
>
> Kahlil Gibran

DIPPING A TOE

Preview: In this chapter we'll ponder the impact of our internal dialogue (self-talk) on our personal development. We'll look at how affirmations can be used to support goal setting and how we can create a more optimistic outlook by the ways that we choose to explain the events in our lives.

INSPIRATION OR DEFLATION

We invest simple words with enormous power; they can build us up or put us down. They can leave us feeling inspired and elated or defeated and deflated. The old saying goes that 'sticks and stones may break my bones but names can never hurt me'. If you've ever been called a **@*%£$!** you will know that this is not true! However, the cruellest words and the most despicable names pale into insignificance compared with the routine barrage of abuse that sometimes goes on inside our heads. These self put-downs can keep us down and they do hurt us. 'You'll never get it right'; 'you'll never succeed'; 'you always mess things up'; 'you are such a screw up'. We internalize the harsh words of others and turn them on ourselves, repeated again and again like an endless loop. All too often they drag us under like concrete galoshes (boots) instead of keeping us afloat like the water wings we wore as children to help us learn to swim. Negative self-talk represents our inner attitudes. It imposes limits on our actions and impacts negatively on our self-image.

The previous chapter had a visual emphasis, whereas this chapter has a verbal emphasis. Here we consider how to *reflect and correct* and rescript our negative self-talk. The aim is to change the running commentary in our heads from inner critic to inner coach. By doing this we create another personal development inner resource that not only helps to support our goals but also helps to create an outlook on life that is more optimistic.

A few years ago I reached a conclusion that made me reel. If other people dared to speak to me in the way I talked to myself, I'd probably never speak to them again! So, let's begin with a personal experiment to gain insight into how you talk to yourself.

PERSONAL EXPERIMENT: NEGATIVE SELF-TALK
Part one: Monitoring your self-talk

Self-talk is like having a personal coach shouting to us from the sidelines, using either words of encouragement or abuse. Before we consider whether we need to make any changes and improvements we need to get an idea of the baseline – that is, the state of affairs right now. The first step to creating empowering inner dialogue is to assess the starting point. This means keeping notes of the kind of words we use. Ideally, one week of data is best for revealing key patterns. However, if this is not feasible then three days is usually enough. You will then have a pretty clear idea of what needs to change.

Personal experiment: Self-talk
Preparation
You will need your journal or a notebook plus three pens: one to make initial notes (blue or black) and two to analyse the results (one red and one green).

Over the next three to seven days:

1   Make a note of every time you say something negative to yourself or, indeed, the times when you say something positive. Note the activity or event that leads to the words' use. Don't analyse at this stage. Just keep notes.
2   At the end of the week, sit down and underline in red ink all the negative words and phrases you used.
3   Circle the positive words and phrases in green ink.
4   Now review this and score each red (negative) item on a scale from minus one (-1) to minus ten (-10), where minus one (-1) is slightly negative, minus ten (-10) is extremely negative, and minus five (-5) is moderately negative. You

are free to use any number along the scale – but avoid fractions because it will make it easier to calculate scores.

5   Do the same for the green (positive) items. The scale for these is from plus one (+1) to plus ten (+10), where plus one is slightly positive and plus ten is extremely positive.

6   This will give you an idea of the overall balance of positive to negative statements.

7   Consider the results. More negative statements (of higher intensity) means that you are beating yourself up and weighing yourself down with concrete galoshes. More positive statements means you are keeping yourself afloat with water wings! The aim is to reduce the frequency of concrete galoshes and their intensity. At the same time, increasing the frequency of water wings and their intensity will lead to self-talk that is more uplifting.

The descriptive words we use to praise or scold ourselves form part of the panoply of self-fulfilling prophecies. We internalize the things people say about us, and these become part of our perceptual filtering. In turn we look for supporting evidence and, before long, we incorporate the words of others into our own internal dialogue.

So, now that you have heard it for yourself and pondered the effects, the next step is to take action to re-educate and rescript that inner voice and change the dialogue from inner critic to inner coach.

Part two: Let me rephrase that
Now that you have the evidence from your monitoring, ask yourself these questions:

- Do the words I use routinely drag me down (concrete galoshes) or keep me afloat (water wings).
- If someone else talked to me in the same way, would I still want to talk to them?
- Would I want to be friends with someone who talked to me that way?

If, on balance, you find that your self-talk is more negative than affirmative, you need to take positive action. Try the following experiment.

Personal experiment: Moral support
- Be your own moral support for the next three to seven days.
- Every time you put yourself down, issue a challenge: 'Would you rephrase that?'
- Use the type of words that your kindly grandmother would, or your best friend.
- Replace the malevolent with benevolent, the bad with the good.
- At the end of the time frame, what did you notice? Does the more affirmative self-talk give you a daily uplift (see Chapter Five)?

The language we use to speak to ourselves indicates our level of self-esteem. It also serves to maintain that level of self-esteem. Once I recognized that I wouldn't tolerate anyone talking to me the way I talk to myself, I knew I had to challenge it and change it. At the very least, we all deserve to be treated with politeness and civility, especially by ourselves!

LOGICAL ERRORS AND COGNITIVE DISTORTIONS

Psychologist Aaron Beck identifies a number of logical errors or cognitive distortions that unfavourably colour our perceptions. In extreme cases these distortions may contribute to psychological problems, such as anxiety and depression. However, we can all learn something from Beck's insights for our everyday lives. These ideas follow on from the self-talk discussed in the previous chapter, but have a stronger focus on our thought processes. Let's briefly consider these cognitive distortions and look at how they impact on our view of the world and of ourselves.

Black and white thinking

Do you see the world in terms black and white absolutes, or do you consider the shades of grey? People who see things in terms of black and white tend to have a high personal need for structure in their lives. They tend to be intolerant of ambiguity and uncertainty. This is often at the expense of accuracy.

Throughout this book we have considered the subject of cognitive economy. Simple black and white thinking is another cognitive labour saving device. Our pre-programmed tendency to seek simplicity encourages quick solutions. Black and white thinking is one of the fundamental characteristics of Western thought (in philosophy). So, we all have this tendency to varying degrees. In novel situations or complex situations the temptation is to go for the simple response, which may not always be appropriate. What we need to do is explore the grey areas to get a picture that is more 'real-life like'.

Imagine a yacht race. The black and white view sees one winner and many losers. However, it is possible for every competitor in a race to win, even though they pass the finishing post at different times. They may not all get the prize, but if they all beat their own personal bests then they are all winners. It's just a matter of perspective. Black and white options represent the extremes of any given situation. Without the grey areas, information is often taken out of context. This leads us to fill in the missing gaps guided with our existing schemas (guided by our perceptual filters). Thus we may jump to premature (and incorrect) conclusions. There is a wealth of possibility and opportunity to be found in the grey areas. Just look for the exceptions to the black and white 'rule' and keep asking the question: 'How else could I see this situation?'

Negative automatic thoughts
Sometimes, negative thoughts seem to pop into our heads – often unwanted and uninvited. Thoughts of unworthiness, and overgeneralizing thoughts that confirm low esteem or failure, are both common examples. The tendency is to rehearse these thoughts over and over again. This is known as *rumination*, which is the psychological version of chewing the cud. Cows keep bringing their food back up so they can chew it over and over again. Cows are not great role models for expanding our view of the world. They also have lousy table manners.

Rumination creates a vicious circle and primes us to look for evidence to support the negative thoughts. To break the cycle we need to challenge those automatic, negative thoughts as they occur and get some fresh insights to chew over!

Logical disputing
Challenging negative thoughts with a logical, questioning approach often exposes the distortions. These are often based on an incomplete picture, a flawed interpretation or a combination of the two.

Firstly, it is important to make a distinction between responsibility and blame. Knowing that your actions (or inactions) led to particular consequences is feedback. Firstly, responsibility is about taking ownership, whereas blame serves no useful pupose whatsoever. Secondly, it's good to get into the habit of considering mitigating circumstances and alternative causes. It helps make sure you are not taking responsibility for things over which you have no control.

So, pick a negative automatic thought that often plagues you, such as 'I'm useless', 'I'm just a screw-up', 'I'm a lousy friend', and so on. Now ask yourself the following questions to test the validity of the statement and expose the black and white thinking:

- What's the evidence for the negative thought?
- What evidence do you have to contradict this thought?
- What are the exceptions?
- What are the mitigating circumstances?
- How do things look from another perspective, such as an impartial observer?
- What evidence would a third person offer to the contrary?
- What exceptions would this impartial observer see?

The aim of these questions is to get more accurate and richer sources of feedback. Often we find that we place unrealistic demands on ourselves and judge ourselves from a biased view. In effect, we set unrealistically high standards and place too many conditions on self-acceptance.

UNCONDITIONAL POSITIVE REGARD
Carl Rogers coined the phrase *unconditional positive regard* for the attitude with which counsellors should approach their cli-

ents. We experience the opposite, conditional regard, every time we get the impression (implicitly or explicitly) that a person's regard for us depends on something we do (or don't do). I cringe every time I hear a parent say to a misbehaving child 'don't do that or I won't love you anymore'. The mistake that we all often make is to confuse the behaviour with the person. It is still possible to love the person and yet not love their behaviour. For Rogers, unconditional positive regard is one of the key necessary and sufficient conditions for personal growth.

However, to strike at the heart of this proposition is, simply, to be more accurate with the language we use, making a clear distinction between the behaviour and the person – in this case ourselves. It's about giving ourselves another chance – not 'shame and blame' but 'try again'. It's about accurate feedback. So, we find that the way we attribute our successes and setbacks has a profound effect on the way we view our actions, our lives and ourselves.

In the next section we identify the different types of explanatory style – that is, how we explain events in our lives and the effect it has on how we view the world.

LEARNED OPTIMISM

People described as 'born optimists' always seem to see the glass as half full. In contrast the 'born pessimists' always seem to see the glass as half empty. However, no one is born an optimist or a pessimist; they are made. Both are learned styles of thinking and perception. We can unlearn a pessimistic style and learn an optimistic one. Although this idea may seem fanciful it is supported by decades of psychological evidence.

In seeing optimists and pessimists as born, not made, we deny the possibility of change. Yet it's clear from research that we all view the world through a series of filters. Running parallel to this we all tend to use stock phrases for explaining the outcomes of events. These phrases act like a kind of habitual script. This means that our outlook is frequently skewed to conform to the script. Martin Seligman, a pioneer in positive psychology, has identified three essential ingredients to these habitual scripts, which he calls explanatory styles. These are: *personalization, permanence* and *pervasiveness.* In order to see how these work, lets consider two average kind of people: Peter and Olivia.

- Peter tends to explain events with a pessimistic explanatory style, which means he tends to dismiss the good stuff and emphasize the bad.
- By contrast, Olivia uses an optimistic style, emphasizing the good stuff and putting the bad stuff in context.

Let's see how the three ingredients of personalization, permanence and pervasiveness play out in their respective scripts.

(i)   Personalization – taking it personally
Optimists and pessimists are polar opposites in the way they explain negative outcomes. The pessimist tends to take it personally, whereas the optimist looks for context and other factors that might help account for the outcome. Imagine Peter and Olivia are competing for an employee of the month award. It's a very close contest but neither of them gets the award. Let's see how they differ in their explanations of the outcome:

NEGATIVE OUTCOME	
Peter's pessimistic explanation:	Olivia's optimistic explanation:
I'm a screw up; it was all my fault.	*It was just a bit of bad luck; other people had a hand in this.*

Peter tends to shoulder the blame himself, whereas Olivia tends to look for other factors.

Now, let's took at how they explain a positive outcome. Both of them were successful in job interviews. Both of them got the job! You'd think they would agree on the explanation of this outcome. Not so:

POSITIVE OUTCOME	
Peter's pessimistic explanation:	Olivia's optimistic explanation:
It was a fluke; I got lucky; it was all down to other people really; it was fate.	*It was down to my personal qualities; it was down to my hard work; I'm good in interviews.*

Even when Peter has a success and should be celebrating, he manages to turn it into a hollow victory. With Peter, every situation is a no-win situation. By contrast Olivia acknowledges her own part in the success. It's perhaps no surprise that Peter seems dragged down by life (concrete galoshes), whereas Olivia appears more buoyant (water wings). Research has shown that there is a link between depression and explanatory style. People who dismiss positive outcomes as change and blame themselves for negative outcomes are more likely to experience depression.

Let's consider another example to emphasize the differences between optimists and pessimists. Peter and Olivia have bought gifts for the in-laws. The gifts were not exactly well received. Characteristically, Peter has concluded that it's all his fault, proclaiming that 'I'm hopeless at choosing presents'. Olivia tries to view the outcome from different angles. She's noticed that other people find it difficult to buy for the in-laws too. In fact the in-laws ('out-laws') often complain about gifts they receive. Olivia concludes that the in-laws are fussy and have very specific criteria for what constitutes an appropriate gift. She'll try to bear this in mind in future but may have to accept that the in-laws just like to moan. This is not to say that we should pass the buck. Adopting an optimistic style means considering the outcome from more than just your own perspective. Self-blaming serves no function except to drag us down – like concrete galoshes. Ownership is about accepting the feedback, learning from it and moving on.

Taken together, the remaining two ingredients to explanatory styles act like a 'hopefulness' filter when following the optimistic script or a 'helplessness' filter when following a pessimistic one.

(ii) Permanence

We all have good days and bad days, but how we explain them counts towards our sense of hopefulness. When faced with setbacks do you routinely see them as permanent or temporary? Do you see successes as permanent or temporary? Again, let's look at the different thought patterns of pessimists and optimists through the eyes of Peter and Olivia. Both of them have had a particularly bad day at work and made a number of mistakes in an important draft report. Usually their work is very accurate. So let's see how they account for themselves:

NEGATIVE OUTCOME	
Peter's pessimistic explanation:	Olivia's optimistic explanation:
I'm all washed up.	*I was tired today (this week).*

We can see that Peter offers a *permanent* explanation whereas Olivia's explanation is *temporary*. This has a big impact on how they recover from the situation. Things will get better. Olivia recovers quickly whereas for Peter it's the end of the line!

The next day at work both Peter and Olivia secure new lucrative clients. Surely this has got to make up for not using the spell-checker the day before.

POSITIVE OUTCOME	
Peter's pessimistic explanation:	Olivia's optimistic explanation:
I got lucky; it was just a good day, for once.	*I'm talented; I get good results.*

We can see that there's a distinct shift in the explanations. This time Peter has gone for a *temporary* explanation, that dismisses his success. Olivia, on the other hand, has switched to a permanent explanation. She focuses on her enduring personal talents. Credit where credit is due and she's not shy in taking it. After all, she did the work!

Now these arc very black and white examples, and it's unlikely that the most persistently 'pessimistic Peter' is going to become an overwhelmingly 'optimistic Olivia' overnight. Before we deal with the final ingredient in our scripts to explain our positive and negative outcomes, let's consider some interim steps for moving toward a style that's more optimistic.

1   Up until now

Every time you find yourself making absolute, permanent statements, closing off any possibility of change, begin by adding the words 'up until now' at the end of the sentence. Then put the sentence into the past tense. So for example, 'I'm rubbish at keeping things tidy' becomes 'I have *been* rubbish at keeping things tidy, *up until now*'. This change in wording and tense opens up the possibility that things could change. It helps guard against those self-fulfilling prophecies.

However, it's still not perfect. The sentence still contains an unhealthy dose of negativity, so let's see how we can neutralize it.

2   Neutralize

Words like 'rubbish' and 'crap' are very subjective and judgemental. Instead, aim for something that is more objective and neutral. For instance 'Keeping things tidy has not been one of my strongest skills, up until now'. This offers hope and room for improvement. You are probably not aiming to be the best 'tidy-upper' in the history of the world *ever*. A satisfactory, workable level of skill may be all you need. It's also important to look out for words you use that impose limits, such as 'I'll *never* get the hang of this'. It could be that things are taking longer than expected, but that doesn't necessarily mean 'never'. Never is a very long time. Instead say 'It's taking me longer than I expected to get the hang of this'.

Now let's look at the second of the ingredients in our explanatory scripts that contribute to our sense of hopefulness (or helplessness).

(iii) Pervasiveness

Pervasiveness is about distinguishing between specific situations and general rules. As before, optimists and pessimists explain outcomes using opposing patterns. Let's see how this works in practice with another example from Peter and Olivia. Both of them have asked someone in their office on a coffee date (they have asked different people). They both get turned down flat. So, how do they react?

NEGATIVE OUTCOME	
Peter's pessimistic explanation:	Olivia's optimistic explanation:
They said no because I'm physically repulsive and have nothing to offer – universal explanation	*I'm just not attractive to that particular person* – specific explanation

We can see that Peter has gone well beyond the evidence. He has come up with a *universal* explanation of physical repulsiveness and that he has nothing to offer. By contrast, Olivia has concluded that the person just doesn't fancy her. Her explanation stays at a very *specific* level. She doesn't go beyond the facts and generalize. So let's see what might have happened had the objects of their attention said yes.

POSITIVE OUTCOME	
Peter's pessimistic explanation:	Olivia's optimistic explanation:
This person is weird.	*I have a lot to offer.*

Again, Peter opts for the no-win situation. He asked someone out, they said yes and now he thinks this specific person is weird. By contrast, Olivia generalizes and considers she has a lot to offer – so why wouldn't this person say yes. Overall, we can see that Olivia's optimistic explanation means that she's more likely to try again. However, Peter with his 'weirdo/repulsive' script is less likely to do so.

By using the same old negative script, pessimistic Peter is always going to produce the same results – that is, a sense of helplessness. Olivia's script by contrast is more likely to encourage a sense of hopefulness. Remember that our world is defined by what we focus on. Let's recap on the ingredients to create hopefulness:

HOPEFULNESS:
- When faced with negative outcomes we need to look for explanations that emphasize that it may just be a temporary situation and confined to one area of life.
- When faced with positive outcomes we need to look for explanations that emphasize that things can be enduring (permanent) and may well spill over into other areas of life.

Being optimistic is not about abdicating responsibility. It's about considering a broader range of options and giving ourselves the benefit of the doubt.

So, what effect would it have on your view of the world and yourself if you adopted an optimistic, explanatory style (Olivia's outlook)?

Overall, this approach is modelled on cognitive-based therapies, which engage the client in finding different explanations of outcomes (more in Chapter Nine). Essentially, strategic questions are used to help us consider more than one perspective on any situation. This helps open up choices for us and thus creates a sense of hope.

Personal experiment: Hopefulness

1   Take a sheet of paper and divide it into two columns.
2   In the left-hand column, make a list of the self-limiting phrases you say to yourself, making a special note of phrases that emphasize permanence or pervasiveness for bad events.
3   In the right-hand column rescript these sentences to emphasize the temporary and specific nature of the situation.
4   Take a moment to imagine the impact on your mood, perceptions and life using the left-hand list (permanent and pervasive). What would it contribute to your overall feel for the day?
5   Now consider the rescripted right-hand list. What difference do you feel? Does it seem more hopeful? What would this list contribute to your overall feel for the day?
6   Following on from the gratitude experiment in Chapter One, look for things that sparkle in your life. Consider all aspects of your life and compile a list. Add to the list every day until you see a pattern of pervasiveness and permanence emerging for the good things in your life.

Now let's consider the subject of luck.

Feeling lucky?

The labels we use to describe ourselves gain power over us. Far from being mere descriptions they become prescription. They dictate the direction of our perceptions.

In *The Luck Factor* Richard Wiseman demonstrates in a series of experiments that the descriptions of 'lucky' or 'unlucky' have an impact on people's luck. In one particular study, after completing questionnaires to determine if they labelled themselves as lucky or unlucky, people were invited to take part in an experiment. The experimenters placed money by the entrance for the participants to find. Everyone had an equal chance of spotting it and yet, on average, the unlucky were more likely to walk past it and the lucky ones find and pocket it. This supports other findings on self-fulfilling prophecy. Seeing ourselves as lucky means that we may be more open to the possibility of finding money in the street. By contrast, unlucky people are hampered by their self-limiting beliefs. This is another reason to keep on doing that gratitude experiment. It keeps the perceptual filters tuned into the possibility of positive outcomes.

In effect, we make logical errors which distort our view. In this next section we consider techniques to address this.

UNDERSTATEMENTS AND OVERSTATEMENTS

How are you today? 'Great', 'good', 'so-so', 'not bad' or 'mustn't grumble'. Why is it that, all too often, we understate our good moods? By contrast, why do we frequently overstate our problems or needs? Why is it then when we want a drink we say we are 'dying of thirst'? Why is it that the mid-morning chocolate biscuit saves us from 'dying of hunger'? Are we not just a bit peckish? And, why is it that disappointment or setback becomes devastation? All of these words and phrases are attempts to communicate our internal states. So, why don't we just say what we mean?

Often we show a bias towards negative or neutral states and underplay the positive ones. Perhaps we feel embarrassed about being too happy, just in case someone else is having a bad day. Conversely, we all like to join in and have a good moan. All too often it becomes a competition – negative-state poker. I'll see your disaster and raise you a catastrophe!

So let's consider a personal experiment to challenge these patterns.

Personal experiment: State your state

1   For the next seven days use words that reflect accurately your internal states.

2   For positive states use positive comments. That means you can't use 'not bad' or 'can't complain'. Also avoid your habitual responses of 'OK', 'fine', or 'alright'.

3   Avoid using the word 'nice' too. It's such a meaningless word! Think of this experiment as an exercise in extending your vocabulary.

4   It's not about being a phoney. It's about creating a wider range of descriptions for moods and states rather than meaningless ones. What exactly do 'OK' and 'nice' mean?

5   When someone asks you how you are, bear in mind the cultural bias for not appearing too positive. So, when in doubt, err on the side of exuberance and crank it up a notch. Just make sure you don't sell yourself short.

6   Perhaps add the word 'very' so that 'well' becomes 'very well'. If you're feeling better than 'good', then perhaps add a 'really' or throw all caution to the wind and go for 'great'.

7   Similarly with your negative comments – avoid exaggerating states for emphasis, such as 'devastated' for 'disappointed'. Be accurate and keep things in perspective. A
broken fingernail, a pimple or coffee stain is not devastation. Reserve 'devastated' for when you have lost everything and everyone you hold dear!

8   *Reflection*: How do you think the choice of language might
affect your moods and mindsets? Do you think people
might relate to you differently? How do you think it might
affect your overall feel for the day? Try this experiment for
one week and find out.

The aim of the exercise is to help expose your habitual (inac-
curate) speech patterns, not to transform you into a grinning
shopping-channel phoney. It is not only famous people who
have catchphrases. We all have stock phrases and idiosyncra-
sies in the way we use language. It's just a matter of becoming
aware that it's sometimes possible, permissible and practical to
push the boat out and *promulgate positively productive prose*. Ah,
that's easy for me to say!

Now let's consider the impact of the language we use on the
attainment of our goals.

GOAL-AFFIRMING SELF-TALK

For good reasons we have a kind of internal alarm system to
warn us of real danger, and potential sources of irritation and
stress. We have probably also internalized messages from our
childhood, such as 'look before your leap', 'don't run before
you can walk' and 'don't get too big for your boots'. At one
level this internal alarm system causes us to give pause for
thought. However, it may be set too sensitively – like the car

alarm that goes off all night because of the touch of a light breeze or passing flatulent rodent.

Our inner critic is our alarm system. It's hypersensitive to failure and often it gives out false alarms as it interprets challenges as threats. We could think of our inner critic as a well-meaning but pessimistic friend who's short on tact. It aims to protect us from harm but tends to use the fewest number of words to get its message across, rather like the old telegraph system. So it says things like:

YOU ARE USELESS. STOP.
IT WILL END IN TEARS. STOP.

Rather than becoming perceptive to possibilities we become impossibly paralysed by perception. Whenever we step outside our comfort zone, our inner critic blurts out stock phrases designed to stop us in our tracks.

To counter our inner critic we need to rescript these stock phrases. So, rather than a stream of unhelpful negative statements, we can replace them with our own affirmative, uplifting ones. Repeated often enough, the new scripts help create balance so that the inner coach can shine through.

An affirmation is a carefully worded, positive statement, which you deliberately repeat to yourself until it takes root in your mind. As another means of retuning your perceptual filters, affirmations can help boost self-esteem, overcome negative self-talk and scripts, and can help support goal achievement. They may be repeated out loud, or written on notes and stuck in prominent places around your home. Affirmations can also be incorporated into relaxation and visualization exercises in order to support our goals. The one-word prayer ('relax') used in the relaxation exercise is the simplest form of affirmation.

However, in order to overcome the ingrained, habitual patterns of our inner critic we need to rescript our affirmative statements in a way that will have the greatest chance of being accepted. Here are some guidelines.

Guidelines for scripting affirmations
The overall aim of affirmations is attitude change. So, to achieve this, they need to be persuasive and hence believable. It helps to link affirmations to goal setting and so the SMARTER acronym can be useful here too. As the name suggests, affirmations need to be stated in the affirmative – that is, positively. To have any power over our attitudes they need to have a personal relevance.

Personal
The easiest way to make affirmations personal is to link them to our goals. This means the goals we set for ourselves, not those which are externally imposed (such as work-based ones). Affirmation should focus on your own changes, not those of others. There are two ways in which you own statements:

1   Put them in the form of 'I' statements, such as 'I am'.
2   Use your name, accompanied by a 'you' statement.

Of course, you may combine both of these approaches by writing two slightly different versions of the same affirmation. For instance, 'Day by day, Gary, you are increasing the percentage of healthy foods in your diet', followed by 'Day by day I am increasing the percentage of healthy foods in my diet'.

Believable

For the affirmation to be persuasive it needs to be believable. It's important to remember that some of your affirmations may contradict your negative self-talk. For instance, you may say 'I'm the most confident person in the world'. The response from your inner critic is likely to be 'Yeah right' followed by 'You have no confidence whatsoever and what's more you're now delusional'. Some self-help books instruct readers to create these grandiose statements, which merely result in inner conflict. As we know, human beings are pattern seekers, and hypothesis driven. As the 'no confidence' hypothesis has been around longer, we will most likely have more evidence to support it. This means that the affirmation is quickly rejected. So, we need a more subtle approach. It helps to use a sense of continual improvement such as 'Day by day I am becoming more confident'. This contains a sense that the change is already happening and is believable. However, it still begs the question 'How are you becoming more confident?' This takes us to the topic of action.

Action-oriented

Affirming to 'tap into the abundance of the cosmos' is all very well, but what are you going to do about it? Linking affirmations to goals makes them action-oriented, since goal setting is about taking action too, not just about wishful thinking. In Chapter Six, we considered the acronym GO-FLOW not 'go with the flow'. It's about taking action to create your own flow. Taking the example of the confidence affirmation 'Everyday with each goal-directed action I take I am becoming more confident'. This is now more believable and less open to dispute from our inner critic. This example also adheres to the next principle of keeping affirmations short and simple.

Short and simple

Shorter and simpler statements take less time to process. They are also less likely to contain ambiguity and less likely to be disputed by our inner critic. Longer sentences with multiple clauses take longer to process. Put two clauses together and it might be possible to agree with one and not the other. Thus, any contradictory affirmation is rejected. It just takes too much cognitive effort to process. Brief affirmations are more likely to be internalized.

Positively worded

Affirmations should *not* include 'not'! This works on the same principle as SMARTER goal setting. If something is phrased in the negative, we first process the positive statement and then negate it. Remember 'don't think about pink elephants'. By the time you've worked out what you must *not* think about, you've already done it. So for instances a phrase like 'I am not shy' is first processed 'I am shy' and then the 'not' is processed. This takes longer and shyness is still emphasized. It is more productive to think of the opposite of shy (confidence) and move towards that! So if you want to improve your diet, it is better to say 'Everyday the percentage of healthy foods I eat increases' instead of 'I am not eating junk food from now on'. If you feel under stress at the prospect of making a presentation, imagine the effects of saying to yourself 'don't get stressed' compared with 'relax'. *Don't tell yourself what you don't want yourself to do.* If you had to read through the previous sentence a couple of times to get the meaning, you'll have realized that it is easy to process the statement 'tell yourself what you want yourself to do'.

Be specific

Perhaps the most famous affirmation was coined by French pharmacist Émile Coué, that is 'Every day in every way I am getting better and better'. The formula of 'every day' or 'day by day' uses the principle of continual improvement. However, it is not specific and not linked to any goal and therefore not action-oriented. What exactly does 'every way' mean? What are you getting better at or what is it that's getting better? *How* is this continual improvement achieved? As it stands it is wishful thinking. Look back at my examples under the 'personal' subheading for increasing the percentage of healthy foods in my diet. If I want to make it even more specific I might replace healthier foods with 'fresh fruit and vegetables' or 'low GI' (glycaemic index) foods in my diet. Rather than 'every way', it is better to write several specific affirmations. And finally:

Values and Strengths

If goals are matched to your values and strengths, then make sure your affirmations are too!

HOW TO USE YOUR AFFIRMATIONS

To use affirmations to change ingrained attitudes, it helps to use them in a variety of ways. This way, they are more likely to be internalized. So try these:

- The simplest way of using affirmations is to write them out ten to 15 times whilst simultaneously saying them aloud.
- You may choose to incorporate them in a meditative practice. After you have induced your relaxation response, repeat the affirmations mentally or our loud and visualize yourself writing them too.

- As affirmations are meant to support your goal setting, you can incorporate them into the future-desired-outcome visualization from the previous chapter. In this way you add compelling words to the compelling images. Top athletes and other high achievers use affirmations in conjunction with visualizations.

Like visualization, affirmations help us to retune our perpetual filters towards positive preferred outcomes. The pattern-seeker in us looks for consistent evidence to support our hypothesis. Visualization and affirmations help us to tune into opportunities, which we can then translate into goal-directed action.

Some people are expert in talking themselves down (concrete galoshes). All that is required is a simple switch in emphasis to talk themselves up (water wings). Same process, same expertise, but with a different emphasis there comes a different result. For some expert negative self-talkers, attempting to use affirmative self-talk may contribute to a greater sense of failure. When initially monitoring self-talk people are often shocked at the extent to which they routinely put themselves down. For others, every time they catch themselves saying 'I'm useless' it becomes proof of their uselessness. They may respond by saying 'See, I'm putting myself down again. I'm so useless I can't even prevent myself from telling myself how useless I am'. Just be aware that judgement is not the aim of the exercise. It takes patience to create new habits, so be patient with yourself. Think of it as a success that you actually spotted it! To help remove the judgement from the process I have devised a simple technique to help you to edit your self-talk. It doesn't require any judgement apart from the ability to recognize a negative statement. Before we consider this process, make a list of your top ten negative self-talk phrases. Then, using any of the principles covered in this chapter, write an antidote, that is, a more self-affirming version.

Negative Self-Talk Phrase (Put-Down) – Concrete Galoshes	The Opposite/Antidote – Water Wings
1	
2	
3	
4	
5	
6	
7	
8	
9	
10	

A particular favourite amongst students is 'I'm sorry I'm being a bit thick; could you explain that again'. As the teacher I respond 'No you're not thick, it's just that you haven't grasped it yet. So I need to explain it in another way'. The question gives me the opportunity to explain the concept in another way which most likely benefits other students and I learn something new too. Let's work with the 'I'm thick' example. We could rescript this as 'I have the sense and the courage to ask questions when I don't understand something'.

Now let's consider the editing process.

Internal editing

Imagine that your self-talk is like a computer program. The negative self-talk needs an update, that is, it needs to be edited and changed to something more productive. This happens with computer software all the time. For the purposes of this exercise let's imagine you are in front of a computer. You are sitting at the keyboard and you can see the monitor screen. It doesn't matter if you don't know where the keys are. For now, just imagine. The process is more important than the fine detail. If you happen to like acronyms I have a new one for you. For those of you who don't like acronyms, I still have one for you, but I've kept it brief: EDIT. This stands for:

Escape, **D**elete, **I**nsert, **T**ype

The idea is that when you catch a put-down (negative self-talk), rather than engage in judgement just say 'EDIT'. This should be enough to remind you of the following process. In effect, it becomes a trigger. Let's consider the four stages:

1   **E** is for Escape – this has got to be one of the most useful keys on the computer keyboard. (with a PC usually situated on the top left-hand side of the keyboard). Hitting the escape key acknowledges that somehow we're stuck, in this case, stuck in a negative mindset.

2   **D** is for Delete – as the name suggests this key is for getting rid of unwanted text, or in this case, unwanted internal dialogue.

3   **I** is for Insert – again as the name suggests, this key is used to insert text. In this case you are ready to insert internal dialogue that is more uplifting.

4   **T** is for Type (or Text) – visualize the new empowering dialogue and say it to yourself in your head (or aloud).

To combine this with a visualization technique, consider the automatic put-down phrases that keep cropping up (from your list above). Then follow these steps:

1   Visualize your negative phrase appearing on your computer screen.

2   Visualize hitting the escape key and then the delete key. Repeat 'edit delete' in your head.

3   Now repeat the words 'insert, type' and retype a more positive phrase. If you can't think of something and the negative comment related to a mistake you'd made, repeat the words 'I'm human and I made a mistake on this occasion. I have learned from the feedback'.

4   Repeat this for all of your negative stock phrases.

Catching negative phrases is a good start but being able to praise yourself is the next important step.

THE GIFT OF PRAISE

Thank-you notes

The ability to accept praise and compliments graciously is not usually thought of as a skill. Many people feel uncomfortable when faced with positive feedback. This is partly due to our inner critic operating in the background. Consider your own reactions to compliments or praise. Do you:

(a) Accept graciously, smile and say thank you?

(b) Say thanks somewhat curtly and move the conversation on?

(c) Mutter an acknowledgement, but do not make eye contact?

(d) Ignore the praise/compliment altogether?

(e) Laugh in embarrassment and say 'it was nothing'?

(f) Put yourself down and point out your faults and failings?

(g) Argue with the person who praised or complimented you and demand that they take it back?

Some of these options may be familiar to you and others may seem alien. For my part I was always rather uncomfortable with accepting compliments and praise and my responses were firmly in the (d) to (f) categories. Two things changed my attitude to compliments and praise. Firstly, on one occasion I pretended not to hear and let a compliment go. However, the other person said 'Sorry, did you hear what I just said?' They repeated the compliment. I too said sorry and thanked her for the compliment. Not long after I heard someone say that praise and compliments are really gifts. Obviously the way to accept a gift is graciously. You still don't have to like the gift. Just acknowledge it with a smile and say 'thanks'. After all, it is the thought that counts. Now I make a point of saying 'thank you'. Of course, I may not always believe it but hey, practice makes perfect. Just by acknowledging the good stuff we can cause a change in our perception of ourselves.

Refunds and returns

Sometimes, however, we may be faced by unjust or unwanted feedback. Surely we don't just have to smile and accept that. Well, why not? I don't always get it right every time but my aim is to say 'Thanks for your feedback. It's not a view that I share but I will give it some thought and get back to you'. Go away, consider the feedback and assess it. Then, get back to them at a later date with your feedback. Tell them you've given it consideration and then what you accept and what you don't. It will certainly take them by surprise. This is also a good strategy for dealing with your inner critic. Of course, if someone is just plain rude, you don't have to accept it. Give them some 'objective' feedback and invite them to rephrase it.

Self-praise is a feedback gift you can give yourself. In Chapter One, I invited you to do the gratitude and anticipation exercise. I'd like to introduce the factor of praise into the experiment.

Personal experiment: Praise

In Chapter One you were invited to top and tail your day with anticipation and gratitude. For this updated version of the experiment, at the end of each day, list three things for which you can praise yourself, however small. As an added challenge, do this when looking in the mirror. Can you look yourself in the eye and say 'well done' and mean it? Do this whenever you achieve something such as one of your sub-goals. It has become a long-standing joke to refer to New Age advocates as 'tree-huggers'. It's easy to dismiss people who embrace nature and hug trees as cranks and crackpots. However, from a psychological point of view it's not the act of tree hugging that matters, it's *the freedom to be able to do it.* Now you may protest that praising yourself in the mirror is silly. However, is that just an excuse not to do it because you would find it difficult? The challenge is to try it every night for seven days. You may be surprised at how much negative self-talk it may throw up. This will provide you with ample material to script your affirmations.

Is this optimism all getting a little too overwhelming?

The good ship Lollipop?

As we reach the end of this chapter you find yourself bristling at some of the suggestions. How could anyone live in a constant state of rose-tinted Pollyanna optimism? Isn't it all a bit Shirley Temple? Isn't the metaphor of water wings a little childish? Well if you find the idea of water wings 'over-the-top' then put on the concrete galoshes! I deliberately chose the water wing analogy because our negative self-talk begins at any early as we internalize what others say to and about us. It also reflects the idea that, as an adult, you might feel foolish wearing water wings. Similarly you might feel foolish or uncomfortable trying out the ideas in this chapter. Nevertheless, water wings work! Perhaps you'd prefer the metaphor of a life belt or a life raft? If so, then own it and use it. The whole idea is that you adapt the material in this book to create a bespoke personal development course (ownership). Positive inner attitudes in the form of affirmative self-talk can give us that all-important buoyancy (and resilience) in life rather than continue to drag us under. Inner attitudes help shape the outer aspects of our lives.

WORK IN PROGRESS

Taken together the four practical chapters in this book (relaxation, goal setting, visualization and self-talk) create a powerful gestalt. That is to say, in combination the whole effect is greater than the sum of the parts. All of the insights offered are with a view to helping you to take ownership of your life. As with all of the information in this book, you have been putting it to the test with your personal experiments and reflecting on the results. Thus the process of refining strategies for positive outcomes is a *work-in-progress*. It is a system for insight, ownership and affirmative action; a personal development strategy that you personally develop *as* you personally develop.

DRYING OFF

Review: In this chapter we have pondered the power or words over moods, mind states and in support of goals. Labels and self-limiting beliefs shape our view of ourselves and of the world. By changing the script we can help change our experience. Although luck is thought of as change we have learned that it is linked to perception, as is optimism. We can all learn to be more optimistic and create a stronger sense of hopefulness is our lives. We also considered the value of affirmations and the guidelines for rescripting habitual negative self-talk.

In the third section of the book we will tie up the loose ends and in the next chapter we'll consider trouble-shooting techniques for eliminating self-sabotage.

REFLECTION (*REFL-ACTION*)

1   **INSIGHT**: What are the three most important things you learned in this chapter?

(i)

(ii)

(iii)

2   **OWNERSHIP**: What impact has this had in terms of the way you think about your accountability for your life and goals?

3   **ACTION**: What action does this inspire you to take to make a positive change in your life? What personal experiment might you conduct to get feedback and insight?

part three:

LESS DISTRACTION MORE ACTION

Chapter Nine

DON'T ROCK THE BOAT!

Overcoming self-sabotage

A well frog knows nothing of the ocean for it is bound by its space. The Spring insect knows nothing of the Winter because it is bound to a single season.

Chuang Tzu

He who postpones the hour of living rightly is like the rustic who waits for the river to run out before he crosses.

Horace

A good intention but fixed and resolute – bent on high and holy ends, we shall find means to them on every side and at every moment; and even obstacles and opposition will but make us 'like the fabled specter-ships', which sail the fastest in the very teeth of the wind.

Ralph Waldo Emerson

DIPPING A TOE

Preview: In this chapter, we ponder the subject of self-sabotage and how to overcome it. A self-sabotage quiz is used to relate problems areas to material in this book. The troubleshooting chapter also includes sections on procrastination and organization issues.

COOPERATION NOT SABOTAGE

When I was at school, one mild form of punishment for disruptive behaviour in class was 'doing lines'. It involved writing out the same sentence a few hundred times such as 'I must not talk in class'. This was rather like doing affirmations only they were invariably negatively phrased and rarely focused on the desired outcome. However, the French teacher did get us to write something very different: 'Co-operation not sabotage'. At the time I doubt many of us dwelt on the sentiment, we were just grateful that it was short.

All of the material in this book so far has focused on how to get all aspects of our lives working together in pursuit of our preferred positive outcomes. If I look back over my life, sometimes I have been my own best friend and at other times my own worst enemy. Sometimes I 'co-operated with my self' and at other times I was my own self-saboteur. The word 'sabotage' literally means 'to walk noisily in wooden shoes'. In this chapter we will consider some of the ways in which we might unwittingly 'put our foot in it' and sabotage our own best efforts.

This chapter works very much as a comprehensive second-chance; a trouble-shooting guide that aims to remove the distraction and get back to action. It targets key problem areas and ways of rectifying them with reference to the material covered in the book so far. It offers feedback to help you review your progress so far and if necessary to go back and adjust your approach. There are also ways to tackle the perennial favourites of procrastination and time management, and the chapter still more tools and techniques for positive lasting change.

Let's begin by using a test to assess the behaviours and attitudes that are self-limiting and self-defeating rather than self-supporting.

SELF-SABOTAGE INDEX (SSI)

For each of the statements, circle the number that most corresponds to your level of agreement. There are no right or wrong answers. The test is purely to put a spotlight on common saboteur tactics.

The test

1   I tend to take things too personally.

4	3	2	1	0
Strongly agree	More agree than disagree	About half and half (agree/ disagree)	More disagree than agree	Strongly disagree

2   I tend to get sidetracked or leave things until the last minute then have to rush to meet important deadlines.

4	3	2	1	0
Strongly agree	More agree than disagree	About half and half (agree/ disagree)	More disagree than agree	Strongly disagree

3   I often refuse to take responsibility for my mistakes.

4	3	2	1	0
Strongly agree	More agree than disagree	About half and half (agree/ disagree)	More disagree than agree	Strongly disagree

4 I prefer to stay in my comfort zone and stick with what's familiar.

4	3	2	1	0
Strongly agree	More agree than disagree	About half and half (agree/ disagree)	More disagree than agree	Strongly disagree

5 I have trouble focusing on my priorities (and values).

4	3	2	1	0
Strongly agree	More agree than disagree	About half and half (agree/ disagree)	More disagree than agree	Strongly disagree

6 For me there are no shades of grey; I tend to view the world in black and white terms.

4	3	2	1	0
Strongly agree	More agree than disagree	About half and half (agree/ disagree)	More disagree than agree	Strongly disagree

7 I am my own toughest critic and often end up thinking 'I could have done better'.

4	3	2	1	0
Strongly agree	More agree than disagree	About half and half (agree/ disagree)	More disagree than agree	Strongly disagree

8 I tend to set myself up for a fall and find a way to 'mess up' before I reach my goal.

4	3	2	1	0
Strongly agree	More agree than disagree	About half and half (agree/disagree)	More disagree than agree	Strongly disagree

9 My fear of appearing foolish stops me from contributing to discussions or asking questions.

4	3	2	1	0
Strongly agree	More agree than disagree	About half and half (agree/disagree)	More disagree than agree	Strongly disagree

10 I often misplace things and then get stressed and angry with myself.

4	3	2	1	0
Strongly agree	More agree than disagree	About half and half (agree/disagree)	More disagree than agree	Strongly disagree

11 I speak to myself in a negative way or put myself down to others.

4	3	2	1	0
Strongly agree	More agree than disagree	About half and half (agree/disagree)	More disagree than agree	Strongly disagree

12 *I avoid taking on responsibility so that people don't expect too much of me.*

4	3	2	1	0
Strongly agree	More agree than disagree	About half and half (agree/disagree)	More disagree than agree	Strongly disagree

13 *I tend not to listen to other people's points of view and often interject with a 'yes but' before they have finished.*

4	3	2	1	0
Strongly agree	More agree than disagree	About half and half (agree/disagree)	More disagree than agree	Strongly disagree

14 *I tend to focus on the downside and expect the worst.*

4	3	2	1	0
Strongly agree	More agree than disagree	About half and half (agree/disagree)	More disagree than agree	Strongly disagree

15 *I give up as soon as the going gets tough, or after the first stumbling block.*

4	3	2	1	0
Strongly agree	More agree than disagree	About half and half (agree/disagree)	More disagree than agree	Strongly disagree

16 I'm prone to jump to conclusions or overreact (based on insufficient evidence) and later regret it.

4	3	2	1	0
Strongly agree	More agree than disagree	About half and half (agree/ disagree)	More disagree than agree	Strongly disagree

17 I hold grudges and seek to get even (for the smallest hurts).

4	3	2	1	0
Strongly agree	More agree than disagree	About half and half (agree/ disagree)	More disagree than agree	Strongly disagree

18 I have difficulty accepting compliments or praise.

4	3	2	1	0
Strongly agree	More agree than disagree	About half and half (agree/ disagree)	More disagree than agree	Strongly disagree

19 I have trouble dealing with criticism, even if it's constructive.

4	3	2	1	0
Strongly agree	More agree than disagree	About half and half (agree/ disagree)	More disagree than agree	Strongly disagree

20 I find it difficult to apologize.

4	3	2	1	0
Strongly agree	More agree than disagree	About half and half (agree/ disagree)	More disagree than agree	Strongly disagree

21 I tend to dwell on negative thoughts.

4	3	2	1	0
Strongly agree	More agree than disagree	About half and half (agree/ disagree)	More disagree than agree	Strongly disagree

22 I look for conflict or react to situations in ways that cause conflict.

4	3	2	1	0
Strongly agree	More agree than disagree	About half and half (agree/ disagree)	More disagree than agree	Strongly disagree

23 I feel I'm a failure if I don't do an absolutely perfect job.

4	3	2	1	0
Strongly agree	More agree than disagree	About half and half (agree/ disagree)	More disagree than agree	Strongly disagree

24 I tend to repeat the same mistakes over and over again.

4	3	2	1	0
Strongly agree	More agree than disagree	About half and half (agree/ disagree)	More disagree than agree	Strongly disagree

25 I let others walk all over me and treat me like a doormat.

4	3	2	1	0
Strongly agree	More agree than disagree	About half and half (agree/ disagree)	More disagree than agree	Strongly disagree

Add the numbers from your responses to give you a total SSI:

Total SSI

The total score will give you an overall snapshot indication of your self-sabotage. Analysis of the individual questions will give you the crucial feedback for the specific areas for further exploration and action. Let's briefly consider the total scores.

Scoring

Low (0 to 30)

You have a great deal of awareness and 'work with yourself' rather than against yourself. You respond to feedback, learn from mistakes and appear to embrace the principles of insight, ownership and action. There may be just a few things holding you back that may have more to do with your perception of the barrier.

Note: if you scored zero, you can skip the rest of this chapter! Alternatively, you need to ask yourself 'Is this good enough'. If it is then likewise skip the chapter. If you feel there is room for improvement, then read on. The choice is yours.

Moderate (31–65)

This indicates that you have moderate tendencies towards self-sabotage. This may mean that you lapse into self-defeating self-talk and behaviours. Go back over the test questions and identify the times or situations when the self-sabotage kicks in. Consider the past three to six months. Forewarned is forearmed. If similar situations occur in the future, you will be better prepared to think about alternative responses that are more self-affirming. There is some indication that you have taken on board the principles of insight, ownership and action.

High (66 to 100)

If you fall in this top range then you really are fighting against yourself. You may have rewritten the script of your life to say that 'things conspire against me' to frustrate your progress. It's time to examine your 'programming' and make the necessary updates. Take time to consider and accurately use feedback.

Learn to find the learning opportunity in criticism. Wherever possible, seek clarification. Use the techniques in this book including visualization for future desired successful outcomes and empowering self-talk. Overall this is a wake-up call to fully embrace the principles of insight, ownership and action.

With your responses to the individual test items in mind, the following pages will help you to analyse self-defeating attitudes and behaviours and replace them with an approach to your personal development that is more co-operative. Begin by selecting one or two items to work on.

The aim of the next session is to explore how these self-defeating behaviours relate to your goals, values and sense of identity. These insights will help you to take ownership and plan counteraction. In Chapter Two we considered the power of reinforcement to condition us to repeat behaviours and to maintain attitudes and thought patterns. So, in terms of its application to self-sabotage, it begs an important question: *what's the pay off?*

WHAT'S THE PAY-OFF?
For each of your selected items consider the following questions. Give yourself time to consider each question and write down your answers. Let's start with two general questions:

1   What's the pay off for these behaviours, beliefs, actions and attitudes? What reward do I get from continuing to behave, think and act in such ways?

2   What's the downside of maintaining these behaviours, beliefs, actions and attitudes? In what ways do they hold me back?

Now let's focus more explicitly on your personal values (from Chapter Three):

Your values

1 In what ways do these behaviours, beliefs, actions or attitudes help me to live according my core value?

2 In terms of your self-sabotage responses, am I living according to my positive 'approach' values or my negative 'avoidance' values?

3 What alternative behaviours, beliefs, actions or attitudes would be more effective in helping me to move towards my positive 'approach' values?

Now let's look at your strengths (Chapter Four):

Your strengths

1 In what ways do these behaviours, beliefs, actions or attitudes help me to make the most of my strengths?

2 What alternative behaviours, beliefs, actions or attitudes would be more effective in helping me support my strengths?

Now let's focus on your goals (Chapter Six):

Your goals

1 In what ways do these behaviours, beliefs, actions or attitudes help or hinder the achievement of my goals?

2 What alternative behaviours, beliefs, actions or attitudes would be more effective in helping me to achieve my goals than what I am doing now?

And finally for this section, let's consider your personal sense of identity (see Chapter Four):

Your sense of self

1   In what ways do these behaviours, beliefs, actions or attitudes contribute to my sense of identity, and towards my self-esteem?

2   In what ways might alternative behaviours, beliefs, actions or attitudes contribute positively to my sense of identity and self-esteem?

Think of this set of questions as a new perceptual filter to help screen out self-sabotage and focus your attention on the 'pay off'. In order to help you pinpoint areas to be worked on, the test items have been grouped under main themes. For each of these, you are directed to material in the book.

WOODEN SHOES

Running, somewhat noisily, in clogs through the self-sabotage test are a number of themes. If we are planning to swim towards our goals, we need to replace our clogs with flippers!

There is an overlap between the categories of analysis with items falling under more than one heading. You are directed to information contained in the book as a basis for counteraction. Let's consider the main reasons for self-sabotage in particular three main feedback, self-esteem and emotions.

Feedback

High scores for the following items indicate feedback problems:

Taking things too personally (1); refusing to take responsibility for mistakes (3); being your own toughest critic (7); not contributing, speaking up or asking questions (9); negative self-talk (11); not listening and habitually using 'yes but' (13); pessimism (14); giving up too soon (15); jumping to conclusions (16); problems accepting praise, compliments (18) and criticism (19); perfectionism (23); and repeating the same mistakes (24).

Objective well balanced criticism, used as feedback, moves us forward but only if it is acted upon. Without application it's about as much use as automatic, knee-jerk, emotionally-laden feedback that sends us off in the wrong direction or keeps us in our 'comfort zone'. It takes practice to deal with all types of feedback and that includes praise and compliments. The 'yes-but filter' blocks the possibility of further feedback and make the problem seem bigger by positively homing in on the negative whilst at the same time negating the positive. 'Yes but' means 'no'. Emphasize the 'food' in feedback. Starvation and regurgitation are not the most efficient routes to nourishment.

There is a crossover with self-esteem issues for many of these items which we will consider next.

Identity, self-esteem, self-belief and self-efficacy
High scores on the following items indicate issues relating to the sense of self and identity:

Taking things personally (1); not taking responsibility for mistakes (3); staying in comfort zones (4); being your own toughest critic (7); setting yourself up for a fall (8); not contributing, speaking up or asking questions (9); negative self-talk (11); avoiding taking responsibility (12); over-reaction (16);

holding grudges (17); accepting compliments (18); dealing with criticism (19); difficulty in apologizing (20); causing conflict (22); perfectionism (23); being a doormat (25). The crossover between the self-esteem list and the previous feedback list is striking. Sometimes it may seem that self-esteem and self-belief are elusive gifts bestowed on the chosen few. However, like most things in human psychology, they are a mixture of learning and perception. The levels of regard (esteem) individuals have for themselves is linked to how effective or efficient the person perceives themself to be (self-efficacy) in different aspects of their lives. With self-esteem, moderation is the key. Low self-esteem may be associated with feelings of worthlessness. However, inflated levels of self-esteem are associated with over-confidence or unrealistic expectations of self-efficacy.

Setting appropriately pitched goals (Chapter Six) that stretch one's abilities with appropriate feedback (Chapter Two) are the building blocks for self-esteem and self-belief and for attaining real life rewards. Self-belief and self-esteem are largely a product of goal-directed living in line with strengths (Chapter Four) and values (Chapter Three). Self-esteem may seem an elusive quality so work on the feedback issues and the esteem will follow.

Emotions

High scores on the following items indicate issues of emotions interfering with feedback.

Taking things too personally (1); getting sidetracked or leaving things until the last minute (2); staying in comfort zones (4); setting oneself up for a fall and 'messing up' (8); not contributing, speaking up or asking questions (9); getting angry with yourself (10); avoiding taking responsibility (12); holding grudges (17); trouble dealing with criticism (19); and causing conflict (22)

Again, there is a crossover with the feedback list and the esteem list. The main emotions apart from 'hurt feelings' are anger and fear of failure. For some people, engineering premature failure represents a small sacrifice for protecting themselves from ultimate failure.

Avoiding unpleasant emotions is one of two main coping strategies. Failure is obviously associated with the unpleasant emotion of fear. *Emotion-focused coping* is an attempt to reduce negative feelings such as in stressful or anxious situations, or even just boredom. Delaying boring or stressful tasks deals with the emotional discomfort in the short term. It's a quick-fix approach. For instance, if you feel a little down, you may rely on your favourite food to give you a boost. The pleasant feeling associated with the food displaces the unpleasant emotion. Alcohol tends to be used in this way too. Although we may often hear talk of the 'addictive personality', more accurately it describes someone hooked on emotion-focused coping.

The alternative coping strategy is *problem-focused coping* or better still *solution-focused coping*. Rather than just dealing with the emotional symptoms this approach requires the person to deal with the problem at source. So if that big pile of paperwork or ironing is getting you down, a bottle of wine, a tub of ice cream or box of Belgian chocolates are not the answers. Rather the solution lies in managing the problem by breaking it down into smaller chunks (sub-goals) and dealing with whatever you can as soon as you can! Setting appropriate goals (SMARTER) can help to limit the fear of failure and to gather accurate feedback. This approach can also help to deal with esteem issues.

In response to the excuse of 'not being in the mood', who says we have to be in the mood for everything all of the time? However, sometimes we don't have the luxury and just have to get on with it. In this situation we can create the mood by using the 'altered states' exercise (Chapter Seven).

Other themes

The other themes in the test are dealt with in the following sections, in particular procrastination (2, 5) and organization (2, 5, 10). The remaining items are used to discuss commonly occurring errors of perception, such as black and white thinking (6) and negative thoughts (21), relating to material in Chapter Eight.

Now, let's consider two main types of blockages that prevent us from moving forward. They are the ubiquitous procrastination and time management.

CALL YOURSELF A PLUMBER?

In the field of personal development are two regularly occurring blockages in the plumbing; these are time management and procrastination. Some people sabotage themselves by not having a plan of action with organized time frames or else let emotions get in the way of getting started. Let's examine the definition of the word 'plumb'. As a verb it means to examine or to investigate. It also means to measure, to understand, to fathom. As an adverb, it means completely, totally, utterly, absolutely, truly, precisely, exactly and right. As an adjective, plumb means upright, level and true. So the question, as we are coming to the end of a book saturated with marine metaphors, plumbing the fathoms of your self-sabotage, is: are you being *plumb* to yourself? If something is 'plumb' it is 'slap-bang', accurate and true. If you are not doing what you say to want to do, then you're not being true to yourself. In fact, you're lying to yourself! The bottom-line (or rather, the plumb-line): *ownership*.

In Chapter Two on feedback and learning we considered Carl Rogers' 'necessary and sufficient conditions' for personal growth. Without a means to deal with procrastination and inadequate organization, the ideal conditions for growth remain out of reach. You have the means to take control. You are your own best resource.

Don't put off until tomorrow what you can put off indefinitely

We are all 'in the same boat'. At one time or another, all of us have procrastinated, are procrastinating or will procrastinate. Have you ever had that extra half hour in bed at the weekend that turned into half the day? Surfacing after that extra sleep, how do you feel? Tired? Leaden? Ready to go back to bed? Have you ever dragged your feet on a project because your heart wasn't in it or because you weren't in the mood? Of course, if we are working to someone else's agenda and pursuing someone else's goals, this response is understandable. However, even when the goals are ours, we may still find ourselves stuck. We put off making decisions or taking action until we really have to. We may argue that we're tired, have other priorities, are not in the right mood, the conditions aren't right, we don't have the right tools and so on. Let's consider some of the reasons for 'not getting on with it'.

Not in the mood

Every time we use the phrase 'I'm just not in the mood' it assumes that we have to wait for the right mood to come along. Of course, this may take a while. In the meantime while we are waiting for the right mood, we could tackle a part of the project for which we don't have any particularly strong feelings one way or the other. Simply break the whole project down into smaller chunks and do the ones that don't require any particular mood. Alternatively, we may just have to 'bite the bullet' and get on with it. Sometimes we simply have to do things when we are not inclined to. It's surprising how the mood comes when we take action. For instance if someone pushed you into a swimming pool right now, you may not be in the mood to go swimming, but assuming you can, you will start swimming! Even if you can't swim, you will do something to get out of that pool, even if it's just shout! Procrastination is really about waiting for that push. However, as we've learned in this book, we do have the tools to change moods at will. Even if we just create a small shift it will more than likely be enough to get us started. Don't wait … Swim out!

In Chapter Four we discussed personal strengths. So often the multitasking approach to personal development assumes that we have to be good at everything. We don't! Are there any aspects of the project that someone else can do? By this I don't just mean getting someone to do the 'crappy' jobs. Are there any parts of the project that could utilize someone else's strengths?

Sometimes we may just need to review exactly why it is we want to tackle a project. Reconsider your motivation in the context of your values and consider the pay-off for completing the task as opposed to delaying it. We need to consider both

the external motivators (tangible rewards) and the internal
motivators (values and strengths).

Internal conflicts
Throughout our lives, undoubtedly, we will experience internal conflicts. We have to decide between two incompatible,
mutually exclusive options. On one hand we may be faced with
approach-approach conflicts. These are the times when we have
to make a decision between two equally attractive options. Either way we win but we also lose out too, as both options are
good but for different reasons. On the other hand we may
have to deal with *avoidance-avoidance conflicts.* These comprise
two equally unattractive options, that is, the proverbial 'devil
and the deep blue sea'. So what is the answer? The first stage
in the process is to conduct a detailed cost–benefit analysis of
both options.

Cost–benefit analysis
This technique is something I use with my coaching clients. A
common dilemma is the choice between staying in an existing
job and accepting the offer of a new one. Both situations have
their benefits but neither is ideal (only for different reasons).
Sometimes it feels like trying to compare apples with oranges.
This exercise will help to weigh up the costs and benefits for
each of the options and quantify them. The result is a pair of
numbers, called *Cost–Benefit Indices* (CBIs). The higher figure
indicates which of the two is the more attractive option. However, in the final analysis, the decision is really up to you. Here
are the steps:

1   Write down a statement of each of the options under consideration on separate sheets of paper. Label them A and B. Divide each sheet into two columns and label them 'benefits' and 'costs'.

2   Consider each option in turn. For option A, in the first column list ten benefits of choosing this option. It can be anything no matter how grand or trivial it may seem as long as you list ten reasons.

3   Staying with option A, in the second column list ten costs of choosing this option. Again, the reasons can be anything from the monumental to the seemingly inconsequential, just as long as you get ten. Now, put this sheet to one side.

4   Repeat steps 2 and 3 for option B.

Although you have lists of costs and benefits for your two options, these reasons don't necessarily have equal value. So, you need to work out which costs and which benefits have the greatest impact for you.

1   Returning to option A, give each benefit an *impact rating* using a scale of one to ten. One means that it has a 'negligible benefit', 5 or 6 means 'moderate benefit', and 10 means that it has a 'massive benefit'. Use any number on the scale to reflect the impact it has for you. However, sticking to whole numbers makes the subsequent calculations easier.

2   Repeat the impact rating process for the costs of taking option A. One means a 'negligible cost', five or six a 'moderate cost' and ten means a 'massive cost'. Now put this sheet to one side.

3   Repeat the impact rating process for the costs and benefits of taking option B.

4   Returning to option A, add up impact ratings for the total benefits and then add up the impact ratings for the total costs. Subtract the total costs from the benefits:

> *Total benefits minus total costs = Cost–Benefit Index (CBI).*

If the number is positive the benefits outweigh the costs, if negative the costs outweigh the benefits.

1   Repeat the calculations for option B to obtain its CBI.

2   You now have two numbers, one for each of your two options. The higher of the two numbers indicates your preferred course of action.

3   Now it's time to make a decision.

However, if the results of the exercise are not conclusive or you can't make a decision, the Solution Focused Brief Therapy approach offers a quick and easy solution for overcoming 'stuckness': flip a coin! Chose one option and conduct a personal experiment! Or, take action to make sure it is the right choice. The cost–benefit analysis approach may also be used to consider the advantages and disadvantages of holding particular attitudes, beliefs and values or the prospect of adopting new ones.

Procrastination through feeling overwhelmed is also an organizational issue. If we don't know where to start, then it means that we need a plan of action.

Never enough hours in the day
Order

Leaving deadlines until the last minute (2), getting sidetracked (2) and misplacing things (10) are all organization issues. They are also matters of discipline. Having a systematic approach to life can be boring for some people, however without any organization whatsoever, chaos reigns! This does not mean a one-size-fits-all approach to organization. It is important that each of us works with our strengths. For instance, I know for my own particular style of learning that I need to tackle problems in short bursts with frequent little breaks and lots of task switching to ensure variety. That reminds me, I'm just off to paint the bathroom! Hey! I figure it's still in keeping with the water metaphor flowing through this book! To the outside it may look a chaotic unfocused approach but it works well for me. I used to beat myself up because I wasn't super-focused in a textbook kind of way. I now realize I don't have to be. I need to continue to refine my approach in line with my strengths (Chapter Four) and my values (Chapter Three). Greater awareness of personal strengths is important as this will help create optimal conditions for each person's particular style of working. In the meantime, consider the pay-off for letting emotional impulses override organization.

Time

Are you one of those people for whom there are never enough hours in the day? Do you sometimes sit down at the end of the day, wonder where all the time went and why you have so little to show for it? Common time management errors include cramming too much into one day and then feeling overwhelmed, or otherwise not establishing clear priorities. To manage time effectively, we first need to know how much

'net' time we have and what we are doing with it. Net time is
the amount of time we have left over after we've slept, eaten,
and performed our obligatory daily ablutions. Of course we
could make a rough guess, but it's important to start with accurate data. To collect the figures we need to perform a time
management analysis. Although it may seem like just another
waste of time, it is always an enlightening exercise. If you've
ever wondered where all of your time goes, this is the surest
way to find out. Just performing this exercise a couple of times
each year will help you 'find the time'.

Time management analysis
For the purposes of this exercise you will need a small note
pad. The idea is that you are going to make a note of how you
use your time over seven days. If you can't manage this, then
just try three weekdays plus a weekend. Start by putting the
day and date at the top of the page. Then, divide the page into
four columns:

Day/date:			
1 Time	2 Activity	3 Energy Level	4 Mood/Intensity

Here's what to do:

1 Make an entry every 20 to 30 minutes, simply noting the time and what you are doing. If you start a new activity make an additional entry.

2 For the 'energy level' column, using the one-to-ten scale rate your energy. If you feel 'drained, tired or wiped out' give this a rating of one. Ten equals 'cup runneth over and on top of the world'. A rating of five or six indicates a 'moderate or satisfactory level of energy'. You can use any number in the scale to reflect your energy. This will help you identify your best times of the day and also those 'energy zapping' activities.

3 For the mood column, just jot down a word that describes your mood. Next to it using the ten-point scale rate the intensity of that mood. One equals 'low intensity', five or six equals 'moderate intensity' and ten equals 'high intensity'. You are free to use any number in the scale. For instance, you may be ironing and your mood might be 'bored'. It's not 'losing the will to live boredom'; it's perhaps just a four indicating 'low to moderate boredom'. This will help you to identify whether the moods associated with the activities are contributing to your procrastination.

Accurate data of how you manage your time puts you in a better position to organize. You may be surprised at the amount of 'wasted time'. The first time I undertook time management analysis I was working from home. I sat down to have my elevenses and the next time I looked up it was time for my threesies! There was a huge gap of time I had filled with various displacement activities. I realized that the four hours I had used in delaying an unpleasant task could have been used to do it and with time to spare!

You may find that simply moving tasks to different times of the day may affect both your mood and your energy levels. Creating a system for prioritizing tasks also helps too. Make a list of the things you need to do, and then assign each one a priority code, like this:

A – means *it has to be done today.*

B – means *you'd prefer to do it today but tomorrow would be OK.*

C – means *within the next two to three days.*

D – means *within the week, and so on.*

E – means *a displacement activity that I choose to do instead of getting on with A to D.*

There are also important questions you can ask to help shift your priorities:

1 Is it really necessary? If so how often do I need to do it?
2 Does this task play to my strengths? Do I have to do it? Could I get someone else to do it?
3 Do the things I spend most of my time doing contribute to my goals, play to my strengths and satisfy my values?
4 Of the things that do not contribute to my goals (and values and strengths), what can I 'let go' or 'get rid of'?

FORWARD THINKING, FORWARD LOOKING, FORWARD MOVING

We learn many of our habitual behavioural and thought patterns by modelling other people. Some of these behaviours and attitudes may have served as defence mechanisms, that is, as a means of self-protection under particular circumstances. We can endlessly speculate as to the origin of our self-sabotage. However, the bottom line is that things change, people change, you have changed and will continue to change. Behaviours and attitudes that kept you afloat at one time maybe hold you back or drag you under right now. This book is not about therapy. It is not about finding the root cause of past hurts. If you think you need to 'get to the bottom of things' then do seek out a qualified professional therapist. It may be part of your learning style to need to know 'why'. In the meantime, however, not knowing the reasons why should not prevent you from making changes and moving forward. Cooperation has an emphasis on co-action, that is, getting different aspects of the self to work together. When considering self-sabotage the overall message is to *unblock or be dammed* (sorry I just couldn't resist the pun).

DRYING OFF

Review: In this chapter we pondered the various ways in which we might be sabotaging our own personal development. We have considered the role of feedback and perception, correcting cognitive distortions and setting co-operation goals. All of this can help to boost esteem issues.

In the final chapter we will expand on the idea of co-operation and consider the power of contribution.

REFLECTION (*REFL-ACTION*)

1 **INSIGHT**: What are the three most important things you learned in this chapter?

(i)

(ii)

(iii)

2 **OWNERSHIP**: What impact has this had in terms of the way you think about your accountability for your life and goals?

3 **ACTION**: What action does this inspire you to take to make a positive change in your life? What personal experiment might you conduct to get feedback and insight?

Chapter Ten

A DROP IN THE OCEAN

The power of contribution

*No [one] is an Island, intire of itselfe; every [one] is a peece of
the Continent, a part of the maine …*

John Donne

*We cannot live only for ourselves. A thousand fibers connect us
with our fellow men; and among those fibers, as sympathetic
threads, our actions run as causes, and they come back to us as
effects.*

Herman Melville

*The community stagnates without the impulse of the individual.
The impulse dies away without the sympathy of the community.*

William James

DIPPING A TOE

Preview: In this final chapter, we ponder what lies beyond
our personal development, the value of 'making a difference', and how an awareness of our social interconnectedness may impact on individual lives.

THE POWER OF INFLUENCE
Casting the net

Happiness is pretty high on the 'must have' (must be) list for most people. The question of how to lead happier more fulfilling lives is an age-old preoccupation of philosophers and psychologists alike. We have already considered, in this book, a number of ways in which we can increase our happiness levels. More relaxation and more fun, changing our perceptions and altering self-talk, living to our values, and setting meaningful goals that stretch us are just some of the ways. But is it the whole picture? Undoubtedly taking ownership and action along these lines will increase our 'happiness quotient'. However, a question that often bobs to the surface suggests that there is something more we can do. That is: *What can I do to make a difference?* This is the focus of the final chapter, bringing together the personal and the social, individual goals and social contribution.

Psychologist Martin Seligman and colleagues have identified three themes for increasing happiness in our lives: *pleasure, challenge* and *meaning*. In the opening quotation, Herman Melville maintains that 'our actions run as causes, and they come back to us as effects'. Making a difference, that is making a wider contribution, can provide new challenges and bring meaning and pleasure to our lives.

So, now we cast the net a little further and consider the prospect and effects of setting contribution goals in a wider social setting.

The social world

We are social animals; other people matter. Our behaviour, thoughts, attitudes and perceptions are in part shaped by our awareness that we belong to social groups. Belonging is part of our identity. Let's consider for a moment a hypothetical scenario that highlights this need.

Imagine waking up tomorrow after a great night's sleep. For once the noisy neighbours didn't keep you awake all night. The moment you open your eyes you just know it's going to be a special day. You make your way to the kitchen to make yourself a drink and switch on the radio. However, there's nothing, just silence. The TV is the same. You reach for the phone to call a member of your family or a friend but there is no dialling tone. Instead, you begin to feel it's going to be one of those days. You nip to the twenty-four hour corner shop for some milk and it's closed! You realize that there aren't many people around. In fact, there aren't any. It's just you! It's as if you are on your own desert island, except that it looks like the physical world you always knew; your social world is no more. No celebrities, no shopkeepers, no lovers, no family, no parents, no children, no colleagues, no friends, no enemies. No social harmony. No social conflict. No social life at all. So, what would you do?

If I was standing outside that corner shop, alone in the world, as a social psychologist, I'd be out of a job, wouldn't I? Well maybe not. Social psychology considers not only the 'real' interactions of people. It also looks at how we are influenced by the implied or imagined presence of others. Even when we are alone our behaviour may be influenced by our awareness that we are performing a role in an intricate social framework. We are affected by the implied presence of others. We are hard-wired for social interaction. It provides an anchor for who we are. So if the self is a product of interactions with others, how can we evaluate our own behaviour in the absence of other people? What would a world without people, without groups and organizations mean for you, the solitary individual? Only your memories of those relationships would be influential and in time their influence would fade, leaving you without any guidelines for behaviour. Part of your identity, perhaps even part of your humanity would be gone. Can you imagine that?

It's easy to forget the bigger picture when we are swamped with day-to-day things. Keeping our heads above water understandably takes precedent over making a wider contribution. Nevertheless, research shows that meaning and contribution are important for our happiness. However, compared with just a few decades ago, we are far less likely to get involved in some form of local community activity. At the same time the incidence of depression is on the increase in the developing world. We may have greater material wealth, but it isn't making us happier. People living in poorer conditions around the world, despite these impoverished conditions, still seem to be happier. Furthermore, we are less happy than our ancestors a generation or so earlier. Perhaps the greater sense of community in previous generations accounted for this. So what would happen if we focused on the social a little more? What difference might we make?

Before we consider this, I'd like to turn the work of psychologist Erik Erikson and his theory of human social and psychological development.

Looking forward to looking back

According to Erikson, as we age our values change. We may think of it like the ripples in a pool. At the moment we splash into the world we have an individual view right at the centre of it all. However, as we grow older and face challenges and goals, increasingly we look outwards to other people. During adolescence our values and perceptions tune in to identity and loyalty. In adulthood we focus on intimacy and love, productivity and care. Increasingly, our focus is drawn to contribution. In our twilight years, we review our lives, our contribution, either from a sense of despair or a sense of integrity of the self. Have we led a life that matters? Hopefully at the end we will acquire the wisdom that befits our advanced age. It is thanks to such psychological insights that 'integrity and wisdom' are not just left to chance. We don't have to wait to make a difference; we can begin taking actions and consider the future desired outcome of our lives, right now.

ACTIONS SPEAK LOUDER THAN WISHFUL THINKING
Karma

The word 'karma' has found its way into many languages across the face of the globe. One aspect of the concept of karma is that our actions have consequences. It is commonly understood to mean 'what goes around comes around'. This can also mean that what we give out will come back to us. It's interesting that focusing on others does bring rewards. People find that symptoms of depression lessen when engaged in volunteer work. Contribution can make us happier.

The word karma means 'action'. Actions of contribution find themselves coming back to the source. So, in this way, the concept of karma fits in with the concept of perceptual filters discussed throughout this book. Our perceptions and attitudes shape our experience and our actions which in turn support our perceptions, attitudes, thoughts, and on it goes. It's said that actions speak louder that words; so does inaction. Our lives get better by the application of insight, ownership, and action.

Contribution goals

So, you've woken up this morning and the world is just as you left it the night before. The deserted streets were just a bad dream. You're so relieved and want to demonstrate your gratitude. What would you say to the first stranger you met? How do you make a positive difference to the world, starting today? Making a contribution doesn't necessarily involve saving the planet every day, it might simply be a commitment to create daily uplifts in the lives of those people on our doorstep.

Personal experiment: giving out daily uplifts

In the first chapter I invited you to commit to giving yourself daily uplifts. Now consider whether you are doing anything that contributes a daily hassle to someone else? Are you missing out on opportunities to give daily uplifts to others? Commit to giving out at least three uplifts to three different people each day. Wherever possible try to make sure they are people you don't usually have much contact with. Make at least one of them a stranger. Try it for a week and see if it's worth continuing. Monitor what effect it has on you. How do you feel at the end of the week?

Making a contribution

Thinking about it, contribution goals are really just extended environment goals. It's just thinking on a slightly bigger scale. It might be visiting people in hospital. It might be writing letters to the local council to improve the area where you live (for you and everyone else). It could be mowing a neighbour's lawn. It might be helping someone on or off a bus with heavy shopping. It could be switching brand loyalty to a company that reflects contribution values. It doesn't have to be a massive sacrifice.

It could be giving all your unwanted items to a charity shop. It could be volunteering at that shop. Do you have spare time to visit people in hospital? It could be applying for grants and funding to improve your area. What about helping someone set goals or share some of the insights in this book?

This may be the time to think globally and do something about your carbon debt: recycling, saving energy or buying Fairtrade. This may be the time to do less driving, get more exercise and so work contribution into your health goals. It could be a time to switch from companies with a bad reputation for ethical trading and write to them to tell them this.

One-off acts of generosity are great, but imagine how things would change if we all committed regularly to contribution goals, no matter how tiny. Think of the difference it would make. With this in mind, what will your ongoing contributions be?

FINDING PURPOSE
Let's begin with the hypothesis that each of us has a purpose in life, that is to be a growing, contributing being. The overall aim of *Don't Wait ... Swim Out!* is to help you realize your personal peak potential growth. So, how do we translate this into contribution? Essentially, it just means taking actions to achieve positive outcomes in a social context. For this we need three ingredients: *action, people* and *goals*. This begs three questions:

1   What is it that you aim to do to achieve your goal?
2   Who do you want to work with to achieve this goal?
3   What is it that you wish to create with these people?

Let's consider each of them in turn.

Action

What is it that you want to do to achieve your goal with other people? Circle words in the following list that appeal to you. There are spaces to add your own words.

help	entertain	reach	teach
assist	guide	enable	empower
validate	lead	encourage	instruct
challenge	prepare	mentor	coach
inform	manage	nurse	enlighten
represent	organize	facilitate	support
liberate	influence	serve	protect

Now consider the following.

People

Who do you want to work with to achieve this goal? Circle words in the following list that appeal to you. There are spaces to add your own words.

audiences	poor	rich	gifted
disadvantaged	ill	men	women
children	clients	minorities	patients
homeless	groups	individuals	nations
congregations	disabled	adolescents	aged
couples	customers	outsiders	peers

Goals

What is that you wish to create with these people? Circle words and phrases in the following list that appeal to you. There are spaces to add your own words.

develop	grow	earn	invest
actualize	laugh	be fit	have fun
be happy	learn	share	prosper
succeed	perform	achieve	think
play	contribute	travel	entertain
challenge	exceed	shine	heal

Select a word from each list to form your mission statement:

My mission is to:
....(**action**)
.... (**people**)
to...(**goal**)

Work with the word lists to create a number of mission statements, and then select the one that has the greatest degree of resonance with your values. Then, use the zero to ten rating to measure the degree to which the statement matches your values and strengths.

Extent to which this mission statement supports values

0	1	2	3	4	5	6	7	8	9	10
not at all				moderately						totally

Extent to which this mission statement supports strengths

0	1	2	3	4	5	6	7	8	9	10
not at all				moderately						totally

Decide what point on the scale is good enough for you. Once you have your mission statement, you can move on to translate it into concrete goals.

BIGGER EXPERIMENT: GO-FLOW

If you have ever pondered the subject of contribution goals, you now have the tools to realize those, as well as your personal goals. So, what effect would it have on your life to include 'connected-ness' and 'positive contribution' in your top-ten list of values?

As an ongoing experiment, use GO-FLOW (see Chapter Six) to set a slightly bigger, medium term contribution goal. For example? Well that is something that should come from you. Try out one of the visualization activities for solution finding and see what emerges. When you have the start of an idea, state the goal and observe what opportunities and choices you may have to fulfil it. What feelings, perceptions or emotions does it invoke? What are your present limitations and how might you overcome them? What are your possible options for achieving this goal? Now, consider: will you do it? When will you do it? Consider how this impacts on other aspects of your life. We are defined by what we focus on, what we value and what we do.

So as we draw close to the end of this journey, I'd like to propose a special toast.

LET'S GET READY TO SUMBLE

The *sumble* is derived from a Viking custom of boasts and toasts made the night before an expedition was launched. It consists of four rounds of toasts, each with a particular theme. These are: *principles, heroes, boasts* and *oaths*. It is not necessary to don the horned helmet and get into your longboat, just a group of willing participants and a pitcher of juice (or water) will suffice. The sumble leader pours the juice (water) into cups or glasses at the beginning of each round. Before each toast begins, everyone relaxes and reflects for a few moments. All should take part on each toast. No opting out.

Principles

The first toast is to the principles or values that each one of you thinks are important. Each person says 'I raise my glass to the principle/value of ...' and then adds a brief reason. From the exercises in Chapter Four, you will have a good idea of what principles or values are driving you. For example 'I raise my glass to the principle of persistence because it is only through persistence that we realize positive lasting change' and takes a drink from the glass, so on for all members of the group. At the end we all raise our glass and say 'Principles'.

Heroes

Next comes a round to toast our heroes or role models. These can be anyone from the past or present that have particularly inspired us. Each one of you proclaims 'I raise my glass to ...', and gives a brief reason and takes a drink, and so on around the group. At the end, all raise a glass to 'Heroes'.

Boasts

The third round pays tribute to our strengths and accomplishments in the form of boasts. Each of you shares something that you have accomplished and are proud of. It is something of a cultural taboo to boast of our achievements, so this toast gives us the opportunity to highlight our successes and provide encouragement to ourselves and to others.

Oaths

The final round is one of oaths, resolutions or goals. Here each of you proclaim what you intend to do. It has to be something that you have control over. You can't make oaths or set goals on behalf of someone else. In turn, each of you raises a glass and proclaims 'I pledge to' or 'I resolve to' and then adds your individual goal. All the work you did on goals in earlier chapters comes in handy here as you focus on SMARTER goals, (that is specific, measurable, achievable, realistic, time bound, enthusiastic and reviewed).

The sumble brings together some of the key themes in *Don't Wait ... Swim Out!* and is a great alternative to the traditional New Year's Eve *Auld Lang Syne*. It can be used any time people want to get together to share insights, inspire and encourage each other in the pursuit of their positive outcomes. It's a great way of maintaining your support network.

NEW HORIZONS: RECIPROCITY

Collectively we contribute to shared perceptual filters about the world. We are bound together in a reciprocal relationship of 'viewing and doing'. What we do in the world not only affects how we view the world but also creates ripples that affect how others see the world. Each of us has the responsibility for changing our own little drop of the ocean. The ripples in the water take care of the rest.

DRYING OFF

Review: In this final chapter we have pondered the power of social influence and a number of metaphors for the interconnectedness of the human race. We have thought about the psychology of making a contribution in terms of its personal impact and looked at the value of setting contribution goals.

REFLECTION (*REFL-ACTION*)

1   **INSIGHT**: What are the three most important things you learned in this chapter?

(i)

(ii)

(iii)

2   **OWNERSHIP**: What impact has this had in terms of the way you think about your accountability for your life and goals?

3   **ACTION**: What action does this inspire you to take to make a positive change in your life? What personal experiment might you conduct to get feedback and insight.

THE OUTRO

Life's a voyage that's homeward bound.

Herman Melville

Thoughts give birth to a creative force that is neither elemental nor sidereal. Thoughts create a new heaven, a new firmament, a new source of energy, from which new arts flow. When a man undertakes to create something, he establishes a new heaven, as it were and from it the work that he desires to create flows into him.

Philipus Aureolus Paracelsus

The summit of happiness is reached when a person is ready to be what he is.

Erasmus

SWIM FOR YOUR LIFE

Water never goes away; it just takes different forms. We may say that we have run out of steam or put our plans on ice. We can cause a stir or make a splash. Water can be muddied, blocked, contained and channelled, boiled, evaporated and frozen but it can never be diluted. Water always contains the solution!

Martial arts expert, actor and philosopher Bruce Lee counselled us to *be water*. We need to make a splash and adapt to forms of the different things that contain us. If we find another container, we have a different experience. Sometimes life's demands shape our destiny, but however it is contained, in essence the water is the same. The most important resources you have are your inner resources, the things that make you you.

Co-operating with our inner strengths takes us forward. We support ourselves by supporting our strengths. When we swim, our bodies, which are made of about 70% water, being slightly less dense than the surrounding water, exert a buoyant force on it. It is relatively easy to stay afloat especially when we are relaxed and allow our bodies to cooperate with the water. It supports us. With the right technique, practice and the application of feedback we propel ourselves forward. As we learn to improve speed so we are able to move farther with the same effort. As we take to water, it takes us forward.

TAKE THE PLUNGE: MAKE A SPLASH
When holidaying in some sunny clime it's interesting to observe the different ways people approach the ocean waves. Some run into the water with passion and dive in head first and others jump in feet first. Some approach cautiously with a temperature-testing toe. The more practical types kneel down to splash themselves with water to prepare for the shock of diving in. Yet others run back and forth alternately chasing and being chased by the waves, summoning up the courage to take the plunge. Amidst the activity others sit by, sipping bottled water, content to be spectators. Some say that they would like to take a dip but have only just applied their sun cream, don't have a spare towel or don't want to lose their spot on the beach. Others wait for conditions to improve and vow to go in when the water heats up, when the sun cools down, when it's not so lively or when the wind dies down. Maybe you are already away

from the beach plumbing the depths of the ocean, exploring a coral reef. Maybe you are just away from the action, sitting it out in the shade of *The Comfort Zone Cocktail Bar* sipping a 'Missed Opportunity'. It's very costly and has a bitter aftertaste from the sour grapes!

If taking the plunge in the ocean were a metaphor for how you live your life, what type would you be? Whatever your approach, the question is simple: are you taking action, spectating or just treading water?

In *Don't Wait For Your Ship to Come In … Swim Out to Meet It* we have pondered the proposition of creating lasting positive change, and springboards, the practical tools and techniques, for achieving it. We have looked at the psychology of attention and perception, learning, values and attitudes, and personal values and strengths. We've carried out personal experiments in the key psychological skills for peak performance: relaxation, goal setting, visualization and self-talk. We have the knowledge and the insight to create watertight action plans to shape our lives. We know how to take control of our moods and mindsets. We know through strategic relaxation that we can effect psychological and physiological change. We know how to create a big, bright, shiny compelling picture of the future and find the buoyant words to do much more than just keep our heads above water. We know that we are part of something greater and through small acts of contribution we can positively change our own corner of the world, by touching the lives of others.

As the cycle of learning continues, and by adapting to the feedback, your perceptual filters will change. Setting goals that help you live according to your values and playing to your strengths maximize the probability of positive outcomes, and will even help you to find happiness along the way.

Undoubtedly, there is so much more I could tell you and so much more you need to know. Part of the joy of living is taking life personally and finding out. It's a lifelong process. Knowing yourself as you do, you get to write the remaining chapters. So what comes next?

MESSAGE IN A BOTTLE
You dream that you are at the water's edge. You notice something bobbing up and down between the waves. You realize it's a corked bottle. This is it! It's the answer you have been waiting for. You dive in to rescue the message. Sure enough inside the bottle is a scrap of parchment. You uncork the bottle and fish out the note written in waterproof ink on special paper. You unroll the note and it reads:

Have a bit of a backlog at the moment.
Sending out my 'the universe helps those that help themselves'
notes.
So, regarding your hopes, dreams, wishes and goals: please start
without me.
Yours wishfully

C.O.

You awake with a start and go down to the water's edge for real, and sure enough you see the corked bottle bobbing towards you, just as in your dream. You uncork the bottle and fish out the note written in waterproof ink on special paper (I added this to keep the sceptical 'yes-but-er' happy). You unroll the note – it contains just three words:

Insight – Ownership – Action

These words are written in your own handwriting. The psychological order trumps the cosmic order every time!

INSIGHT, OWNERSHIP AND ACTION

Throughout this book we have considered the principles of *insight, ownership* and *action*. They are the star-like ideals that mariners can use as guides to navigate stormy waters to reach their destiny. This is so because they require us to look within ourselves to the essence of our shared human psychology and the unique patterns of our individual values and strengths. These principles give meaning to the (paraphrased) words of William Shakespeare who said 'It is not in the stars to hold our destiny but in ourselves'.

In the final analysis, we can choose to live in the dreamy twilight world of 'what if' or 'if only' but the question that begs an answer is 'what about now?' Now that you have gained the insight and taken ownership of your goals, when do you take action? The answer can only be: now!

The words of Marie Beyon Ray sum it up beautifully:

Begin doing what you want to do now. We are not living in eternity. We have only this moment, sparkling like a star in our hand and melting like a snowflake. Let us use it before it is too late.

Don't wait for fate. Don't wait for your ship to come in: swim out to meet it. Do it now. Make a splash! Swim for your life! It's closer than you think.

Gary Wood

FURTHER READING AND RESOURCES

This section provides a selected annotated resource and reading list rather than an exhaustive bibliography. As with any self-help book, the secret lies not in the reading but in the insight, ownership and action.

All links for websites were tested at the time of writing. Some of the links are a bit convoluted so type them carefully.

THREE INSPIRATIONAL NOVELS

Together these three books have been a constant source of inspiration. Every time I read them I get something new. I recommend that you read them in this order:

1   Antoine de Saint-Exupéry, *The Little Prince* (Kathryn Woods translation), Picador Books, London, 1982
2   Richard Bach, *Jonathan Livingston Seagull: A Story*, Harper-Collins, 1994
3   Richard Bach, *Illusions: The Adventures of A Reluctant Messiah*, Arrow Books, 2001

FILMS

Here are three films which tie in with the themes of perceptual filters and contribution:

1   *Pleasantville* (1998, directed by Gary Ross)
2   *Big Fish* (2003, directed by Tim Burton)
3   *Pay it Forward* (2000, directed by Mimi Leder)

CREATIVE VISUALIZATION

Steve Andreas and Charles Faulkner, *NLP: The New Technology of Achievement*, Nicholas Brealey Publishing, London, 1996

This is a comprehensive guide to NLP and contains numerous visualization techniques. Although undoubtedly useful for changing perceptual filters, do take the claims of instant change with a pinch of salt. These results remain unsupported by research into comparative outcomes.

Shakti Gawain, *Creative Visualization*, Bantam Books, London, 1982
This little book offers the most concise introduction to creative visualization, although it does have a 'New Age' spiritual tone. Anyone familiar with Cosmic Ordering will be struck by the similarities.

Maxwell Maltz, *Psycho-Cybernetics*, Pocket Books, London, 1969
This book, originally published in 1960, has been extremely influential in sports psychology and personal development in general. It has a more pragmatic, down-to-earth tone than many personal development books. Unfortunately some of the case studies are dated. Some motivational gurus ruthlessly 'borrow' from this work.

GOALS
Mihalyi Csikszentmihalyi, *Flow: The classic work on how to achieve happiness*, Rider, London, 2002
It says it all in the title. It's an evidence-based review of goal setting and the implications – happiness!

MEDITATION
David Fontana, *Learn to Meditate*, Duncan Baird Publishers, London, 1999
This is a colourful basic all-round introduction to meditation.

RELATIONSHIPS

Riane Eisler, *The Chalice and the Blade: Our History, Our Future*, HarperCollins, San Francisco, 1987
A fascinating book that offers a journey through history and describes a way of life based on partnership, equality and harmony with nature. Well worth a read.

Riane Eisler, *The Partnership Way: Seven Relationships That Will Change Your Life*, New World Library, 2002
This offers practical guidance based on the partnership philosophy outlined in *The Chalice and the Blade*. It has an emphasis on US social and political structures, but most of the book has international applications.

Gary W. Wood, *Sex, Lies & Stereotypes: Challenging Views of Women, Men and Relationships*. New Holland, London, 2005
This book challenges gender stereotypes and offers a more co-operative, partnership view of relationships. If offers a tour through evidence from a range of disciplines including theology, psychology and philosophy. Well worth a read, even if I do say so myself.

CONTRIBUTION

Ultimately we are all in this together and so a percentage of the author's profits will be donated to charities that help people who face enormous obstacles in life through no fault of their own. Although you may already have your own list, here are a few 'contribution' books and websites to consider:

Books

Masuru Emoto, *The Hidden Messages in Water*, Pocket Books, London, 2005
This inspirational little book contains a number of water photographs together with a treatise on the power of contribution. I use it merely as a metaphor, not for the unsupported 'science'.

Michael Norton, *365 Ways to Change the World*, Harper Perennial, London, 2006
Something to do for everyday of the year.

Change the World for a Fiver: We Are What We Do, Short Books, London, 2004
This book costs a fiver (£5 sterling) and contains a wealth of ideas for making a difference, presented in a fun and accessible way.
See also Riane Eisler under Relationships.

Websites

Here's a short list of contribution websites:

Amnesty International: http://www.amnesty.org/
Fairtrade: http://www.fairtrade.org.uk/
G.I.F.T http://www.giveitforwardtoday.org/
Oxfam: http://www.oxfam.org.uk/
Unicef: http://www.unicef.org/

SELF-TALK

Martin E. P. Seligman, *Learned Optimism: How to Change Your Mind and Your Life*. Free Press, London, 1998
This offers a summary of Seligman's work in the field of helplessness and optimism, including a full psychometric test and

directions for creating an outlook that is more optimistic. It is a must read.

STRENGTHS
Books

Marcus Buckingham and Donald O. Clifton, *Now, Discover Your Strengths*. Pocket Books, London, 2004
This book focuses on strengths in a work setting and has a one-off access to an assessment questionnaire. The one downside to the Buckingham and Clifton approach is that the online assessment questionnaire accompanying their book is a one-shot deal and the resulting top five strengths are deemed to be fixed for life. However, assertion is arguably more to do with protecting copyright than having a strong psychological basis.

Martin Seligman, *Authentic Happiness*, Nicholas Brealey Publishing, London, 2003
This offers psychometric tests to determine character strengths and proposes the idea that we can increase our happiness by living to them.

Website

For Martin Seligman's *Authentic Happiness* homepage containing numerous online self-assessment questionnaires, go to: http://www.authentichappiness.sas.upenn.edu/

BREATHING

Loehr, James, E. and Midgow, J.A., *Breathe in, breathe out: inhale energy and exhale stress by guiding and controlling your breathing*, Time-Life Books, Alexandria, Virginia, USA, 1986 and 1999

A comprehensive coverage of different types of breathing techniques.

COURSES

Personal development courses and coaching

I offer a number of short personal development courses some of which are based on this book. I also offers personal development coaching, both face-to-face and by telephone. Courses include: *Psychological Skills for Peak Performance and Positive Outcomes*; *Advanced Goal setting*; *Team Building*; *Gender and Relationships*; *Communication Skills*; *Relaxation and Creative Visualization*; and others.

For further details see: www.drgarywood.co.uk or www.psy-central.co.uk.

Creative visualization

As a psychologist I have studied The Silva Method as a way of deepening my understanding of creative visualization techniques. Conventional science does not necessarily support the entire theoretical basis for the method or for its claims of efficacy. However the courses offer a relaxation method and techniques for the creative use of the imagination. It is on this basis that I offer the following links:

- For details on the Silva Method dynamic meditation and creative visualization course worldwide go to: www.silvamethod.com
- For details of courses in the UK go to: www.silvamethod.co.uk

Breathing, yoga and meditation

Art of Living Course (www.artofliving.org)

An intensive course run internationally, teaching breathing and meditation techniques. Whilst I do not necessarily subscribe to all of the philosophy, I found the breathing exercises very useful.

LEARNING
Books
Bill Lucas, *Power Up Your Mind. Learn faster, work smarter*, Nicholas Brealey Publishing, London, 2001
A comprehensive guide to improving learning.

Websites
These online tests will be useful in helping you to understand yourself as a learner. Some of the links include tips and strategies for becoming more flexible in your approach to learning. For further information search for 'learning styles' or type in the heading of the tests in your web search engine.

There are numerous free resources on the web to allow you to explore your learning styles. Many of them require you to sign up using an email address. I recommend that you set up an email address especially for your personal development.

All links were live at the time of writing.

Index of Learning Styles (Soloman & Felder) (highly recommended):
- http://www.engr.ncsu.edu/learningstyles/ilsweb.html
- http://www.crc4mse.org/ILS/self_test.html

Canfield's learning styles inventory
http://www.tecweb.org/styles/canfield1.html

VARK questionnaire
http://www.vark-learn.com/english/page.asp?p=questionnaire

Learning Styles Inventory
http://www.rrcc-online.com/~psych/LSInventory.html

Honey and Mumford's Learning Styles Questionnaire
http://www.peterhoney.com/product/brochure

CRITICAL SOURCES
The field of personal development is something of a mine-field. Sources vary enormously. Here are some critical sources to help you explore matters in greater depth.

Books
Steve Salerno, *Sham. How The Gurus of the Self-Help Movement Make Us Helpless*, Nicholas Brealey Publishing, London, 2005
This book begins by examining the problems with the self-help movement but descends into a political right-wing rant. So, just read the first half and take the second with a generous pinch of salt.

Websites
- To check out Quackwatch go to: www.quackwatch.org/
- To check out the Skeptics Dictionary which contains entries on many New Age phenomena go to: www.skepdic.com

ABOUT THE AUTHOR
You can find out more about me by visiting my website at: www.drgarywood.co.uk.

FOR YOUR *DON'T WAIT FOR YOUR SHIP TO COME IN ...*
SWIM OUT TO MEET IT **COCKTAIL PARTY**
Nostalgia-themed nights have become popular at clubs so I
thought I'd offer a select playlist for your own cocktail party.
I've included songs from different genres and eras. Some of
them will be familiar to you and some of them may be new.
There's something in there for everyone, but do feel free to
add your own 'water-themed' and 'positive-outcome-themed'
favourites.

The music
- Bridge Over Troubled Waters – Simon and Garfunkel
- Cry Me a River – Justin Timberlake
- Don't Stop – Fleetwood Mac
- Don't Stop Me Now – Queen
- Good Vibrations – The Beach Boys
- I Am What I Am – Gloria Gaynor
- I Will Survive – Gloria Gaynor
- In the Navy – Village People
- Islands in the Stream – Dolly Parton and Kenny Rogers
- Let the River Run – Carly Simon
- Many Rivers To Cross – UB40
- Maybe This Time – Liza Minelli
- Message in a Bottle – Police
- My Ship is Comin' In – Walker Brothers
- On the Good Ship Lollipop – Shirley Temple
- Orinoco Flow (Sail Away) – Enya
- River Deep, Mountain High – Ike and Tina Turner
- River of Dreams – Billy Joel
- Sail Away – David Gray
- Sailing – Rod Stewart

- Sailing on the Seven Seas – OMD
- Sea Cruise – Marc Bolan/T.Rex
- Something Good – Utah Saints
- SOS – Abba
- SOS – Rhianna
- Splish Splash – Bobby Darin
- Sweet Dreams (Are Made of This) – Eurythmics
- Take Me To The River – Annie Lennox
- Things Can Only Get Better – D:Ream
- We Are The Champions – Queen
- We're All Water – Yoko Ono
- When the Going Gets Tough – Billy Ocean

The cocktails
Here are a few suggestions for *Don't Wait for Your Ship to Come In … Swim Out to Meet It* cocktails:

The Colin Cherry
1 measure of each:
Southern Comfort
Cherry Brandy
Sweet and Sour Mix
1 dash of grenadine
Top up with cranberry juice to serve in a tall glass

Doctor Good Life
Equal measures of:
Southern Comfort
Crème de Cacao
Banana liqueur
Butterscotch Schnapps

Dash of cream
Sprinkle of nutmeg

Beyond the Blue
Equal measures of:
Southern Comfort
Blueberry Schnapps
Blueberry Vodka
Blue Curacao
Served in a tall glass with lots of ice

Shirley Temple (Non-alcoholic)
Tall glass
Ginger ale
Grenadine Syrup
Orange Juice
Garnished with a maraschino cherry and slice of lemon
Variations: the orange juice is often omitted and the ginger ale
is replaced for lemon-lime fizzy soft drink

Missed Opportunity
Take a tall glass and coat the wet rim with salt
Small glass of the driest white wine you can find
Top up with grapefruit juice and bitter lemon
Add a good jigger of angostura bitters
A dash of vinegar
Top with a couple of dead flies (or live ones – they'll try to fly
through the sides of the glass)
Serve at room temperature

Whatever you do; don't drink it! Just imagine what the fabulous cocktails taste like of the people around you

The Positive Outcome Metaphor
Long, tall, cool glass of pure water

Cosmic Order
Take one empty glass ... and wait!

The poem: Desert Island Discovery
Palm tree-lined beaches frame the tranquil azure sea.
Stroll in the sun with the crisp white sand beneath your feet.
Calmed by the soothing lullabies of some exotic bird as twilight ushers in,
The gentle cooling breeze against your sun-kissed naked skin.
And so you dream the dreams of angels, gods and kings.
Re-live the wonder that each new passing day will bring.
The palm tree-lined beaches.
Dive into a tranquil azure sea.
Strolling in the sun, the crisp white sand beneath your feet.
As each night the plaintive lullabies of strange birds usher in,
The twilight cooling breeze against your sun-bronzed naked skin.
Awaken to the day of trees and beaches, sun and sea,
Running through the hot white sand with aching feet,
Another night disturbed by strange birds' mawkish din,
The chilling wind intensifies the pain of sunburnt skin.
Vividly in nightmares the horror of each day repeats,
Burning sun and sand and glaring sea, infected, raw and blistered feet.

Inhuman cries of threatened doom punctuate the hostile murk,
With no respite throughout each night, you dream to spend a day at work.
Familiar faces met each day, the jokes to while the time away,
Working well into the dark, the concrete building grey and stark,
Water fountain, potted palm, stressed out people dream of calm,
Ah! It would be so very nice,
A desert island paradise.

APPENDIX

PERSONAL EXPERIMENT REPORT

Hypothesis: What do I want to find out?
What will I do? When?
What resources will I need?
Do I need anyone to help me? If so, who and how?
What are the results?
What are my conclusions?
What are the implications for future personal experiments?
What will I do next?

GRATITUDE AND ANTICIPATION EXPERIMENT

Day no:	
Gratitude (evening): *What was I grateful for today? To whom was I grateful?*	
Things	1
	2
	3
People	1
	2
	3

Anticipation (morning):
Tomorrow, what am I looking forward to?

1	
2	
3	
Notes:	

ACTION PLAN: GO-FLOW

Goal:
(Stated using SMARTER)

Observation:
(opportunities, reality and choices)

Feelings:
(checking your feelings, perceptions, emotions and attitudes to the goal)

Limitations/Let-Downs:
(considering what the limitations are for this goal, how you can counter them and how you will deal with let-downs)

Options:
(considering all possible options of achieving the same outcome)

Will – I will do it:
(statement of intent)

GOAL SETTING ACTION PLAN

Your goal (using SMARTER)

Is it short-, medium-, or long-term ....

Estimation of time scale .... months/years

Reasons for wanting to achieve this goal:

1

2

3

4

5

* NOW – Do the Future Desired Outcome exercise

Commitment to achieving your goal: On a scale of 1 to 10, rate your commitment to achieving your goal:

1	2	3	4	5	6	7	8	9	10
Little/no commitment ←――――――――――→ Total commitment									

If not 10, what do you need to do to increase your commitment?

> **Review reasons/Repeat 'Future Desired Outcome' Exercise/How will you celebrate?**
>
>
>
>
>
> **Declaration of commitment**: *Signed* ....
>
> *Date*..

What obstacles do you need to overcome to achieve your goal?

Obstacle	Solution
1	
2	
3	
4	
5	

Milestones to achieving overall goal

Milestones/sub-goals	Target date	Date achieved
1		
2		
3		
4		
5		
6		
7		
8		
9		
10		
Overall target date		

Note: Spend a few minutes reading your written goal daily, reviewing the reasons why you want to achieve it. Regularly repeat the *Future Desired Outcome Exercise.*

Remedial action: Are you on course?

Goals often need fine-tuning or adjustment, so if your target date is looking unrealistic, what actions do you need to take?

1

2

3

4

5

Option to set new target date:

OTHER NOTES/REFLECTIONS/FEEDBACK:

What have you learned about goal setting that will help you when setting your next goal?

JOURNAL NOTES:

INDEX

values, 66, 268
    avoidance type, 75, 76, 79, 80, 81
    approach type, 68, 75, 80
    instrumental, 67
    terminal, 67
values exercise, 68
vicarious learning, 48
visualization, 184, 185, 188, 189,
        193, 200, 202, 241, 246, 249,
        253, 267, 295, 307, 311
    persistence, 202
    positive reinforcement, 202
    problem solving, 205

water, 7, 58, 113, 154, 159, 189, 190,
        191, 297, 300, 301, 309
weaknesses, 96
what's the pay-off?, 267
Whitmore, John, 170
Willis, Bruce, 8
Wiseman, Richard, 238
wishful thinking, 179, 243, 245
Wood, Gary, 308
wooden shoes, 269
WYSIWYG, 31

yes-but, 32, 270